SOUTHERN ILLINOIS UNIVERSITY PRESS
Carbondale and Edwardsville

Rescuing the Subject

A Critical Introduction to Rhetoric and the Writer

Susan Miller

4   3   2   1   92   91   90   89

Library of Congress Cataloging-in-Publication Data

Miller, Susan
    Rescuing the subject : a critical introduction to rhetoric and the
    writer / Susan Miller.
        p.   cm.
        Bibliography: p.
        Includes index.
        1. English language—Rhetoric—Study and teaching.   2. Rhetoric.
    I. Title.
    PE1404.M554   1989   88-18196
    808'.042'07—dc19   CIP
    ISBN 0-8093-1501-7

The paper used in this publication meets the minimum
requirements of American National Standard for information
Sciences—Permanence of Paper for Printed Library Materials,
ANSI Z39.48–1984. ∞

Contents

vi   Contents

Acknowledgments

In the time that this book has been in the works, I have had generous support that demonstrates one of its theses— that writing is never only the result of single "authorship" or of private insight. I want to express my gratitude to my collaborators as fully as I can, unaware as they have been of the exact role of many of their contributions.

I am indebted to the University of Wisconsin-Milwaukee College of Humanities and Center for Twentieth-Century Studies for a Senior Research Fellowship in 1982, during which another Fellow, Stephen Watson, was willing to talk endlessly about theoretical issues raised in his work on the philosophical problem of the subject. The National Endowment for the Humanities provided a Summer Stipend in 1983 that allowed me time to draft chapter 3 of this study in England. There Stephen Tchudi, Harold Rosen, and David Allen also helped, in ways they were not aware of, as I focused on the implications of writing instruction in British schools and came to understand continuing British social emphases on elocution. John Manners of Blackwell's Rare Books in Fyfield was particularly helpful in turning up copies of early rhetorics and schoolbooks, and Richard Sterling of Herbert H. Lehman College, New York, willingly contributed his unique Anglo-American perspective on the teaching of writing. In addition, I am grateful to the University of Utah College of Humanities for two research leaves, during which I have completed this manuscript, and especially to Dean Norman Council for providing another administrator time to write.

During this long process, my colleagues in Wisconsin and Utah have been extraordinarily patient and helpful discussants and commentators on the issues addressed here. Herbert Blau's performance theory, Henry Staten's philosophical perspective on Derrida and Wittgenstein, and Robert Cas-erio's good cheer and insightful comments all appear here as subtextual underpinnings for this study.

Many other colleagues, students, and friends read various versions of the manuscript and made invaluable contributions to its current form. Joseph Williams, Gretchen Flesher, Kathy Fitzgerald, Ann Berthoff, David Bartholomae, Andrea Lunsford, and Sara Garnes have devoted much valuable time to arguing with, improving, and testing substantial portions of the book. Dean Rehberger and especially Elizabeth Larsen, whose dissertation research about the history of composing processes I both guided and followed, have asked questions and provided sources without which I would not have been able to complete this study. In particular, Elizabeth's doctoral work first quoted many of my historical citations. Sylvia Morris and Laurel Brown have also helped by giving more than secretarial help to the many versions of each section.

I am also deeply indebted to Nicole Hoffman for her many substantial and formal contributions, as I am to Bill Irmsher and Lisa Ede, who reviewed the manuscript. They and Kenney Withers lent invaluable support from a uniquely appropriate press.

Salt Lake City, Utah

Rescuing the Subject

Introduction

Those of us whose primary professional interest is composition and student writing are well aware that "composition and rhetoric" is the most common name given to our field. We take many positive benefits from this combination, not least of which is the historical legitimacy and continuity that rhetorical studies appears to give our work. It is common to assume that composition is at least an indirect descendant of an earlier rhetoric, broadly defined as an ancient and continuing set of principles about the shaping and production of effective discourse. We loosely equate the purposes and theory of instruction we give to contemporary students with practices in rhetorical education and in the advanced study of discourse that has been theorized and taught in many versions since the Greek Academy.

But explaining how our contemporary study of writing is related to an ancient and continuing art of discourse is more complicated than applying the label "composition/rhetoric" to what we do. Theoretical and practical relationships between disciplines of rhetoric and of written composition are not at all clear in popular names for the field, a fact that has been obvious in the debate following the publication of Cy Knoblauch and Lillian Brannon's book, *Rhetorical Traditions and the Teaching of Writing*.[1] We need to follow the direction implied by this debate, to reevaluate the place of classical theories in contemporary teaching. But this book argues that both the debate occasioned by Knoblauch and Brannon's work and the larger reevaluation of which it is part have progressed without a necessary, but prior, account of how actual acts of writing comment on both rhetoric and composition.

By this I mean that those of us in composition have a great deal at stake in rereading the history of rhetoric and its

1

related fields in light of our chief concern, the act of writing. Our sense of ourselves as participants in a coherent, discrete discipline and our expertise about the primary objects of study in that discipline—the identity and the acts of writers—depend on creating a clearer sense than we now have of the historical inevitability of a contemporary field of *written* composition. Historical impulses toward and against theorizing written discourse and formally organizing its pedagogy reveal a great deal about composition's currently blurred relations to formal rhetoric. But these contrary impulses also clarify composition's "place" among realist philosophical traditions that fundamental grounds for rhetoric have unsuccessfully opposed. They similarly help explain the field's stature in a broadly defined history of discourse education that can include literary studies.

To highlight the writer and the act of writing in a rereading of historical rhetoric, its philosophical embedments, and the progress of discourse education, I have assumed that contemporary composition studies is an inevitable cultural outcome from changing conditions for discourse production. None of the intellectual domains with which we concern ourselves, including rhetoric, philosophical commentary on it and on written language, literary and literacy theory, and discourse pedagogies, have been produced independently of social and material circumstances for writing. But we have not yet accounted for our intellectually discrete study of writers and their acts in terms of this relevant but often mislaid history of the changing act of writing. Nor have we kept an eye to the multiple identities of writers, which changes in conditions for writing have incrementally accumulated. Our intellectual relations with similar fields as well as the inevitability of our recent separations from them have, consequently, remained unclear.

To speak in immediately practical terms of the difficulties that this blurring gives us, we can turn to some problems that the growth of composition studies has not overcome. The study of written composition not only is persistently defined and redefined as an offshoot of a rhetoric conceived in, and for, oral interactions but is also subordinated to full literary awareness and to its parallel, complex, and independent liter-

[handwritten margin note: lack of comp philosophy]

acy. Composition studies has not yet claimed its purchase on philosophical positions that place written language and its necessary uncertainty above rhetoric's claims to control and analyze the direct impact of an utterance, and above formalist literary theories that claim to perceive and explain clear "meanings." Nor has the field fully conceived of the literate person as a "writer," who may or may not be an "author," a source of writing whose full participation in culture depends on an active yet ambivalent relation to all written texts. But placing conditions for acts of writing and the nature of a multiply defined "writer" in the center of composition theory and practice would address our subsidiary intellectual status. It would, that is, explain all writing and writers from a historically empowered perspective on actual motives for, conditions around, and constraints on acts of writing and their results.

[handwritten margin notes: don't I do this? / the dev]

If we value writing this highly, placing its history of technological developments and their call for redefinitions of its human instruments in the foreground of history, theory, and practice, we become able to rewrite much intellectual history, especially the history of rhetoric, without strains of regret about a "decline" or "fragmentation" of what is still primarily imagined as oral discourse. Changing technologies for discourse production and their accumulated contributions to defining a contemporary writing "subject," the human source of texts, refresh this regretful history. These changes and contributions also call for a welcomed new textual rhetoric that composition studies might assertively own. But, equally important, a reformed vision of how specifically written discourse originates can rescue a concept of the "subject" or "author" of writing from its currently precarious theoretical and philosophical place. We can, that is, explain historically why it remains feasible to investigate the human "writer" without necessarily surrounding that person with the now easily deniable claptrap of inspired, unitary "authorship" that contemporary theorists in other fields have so thoroughly deconstructed. By clarifying our own stance toward the writer and the history relevant to that position, we demonstrate that composition now has a historically mandated explanatory role among other textual studies.

[handwritten margin notes: Bakhtin / Plato]

I have approached this rereading from a recursive,

rather than linear, perspective. Instead of starting at the beginning of what we take to be Western discourse history and
ending with the establishment of composition, I have chosen
to take a thematic approach. Since I am claiming that writing
comments, and has always commented, on a group of intellectual domains—rhetoric, philosophy, literary and literacy studies—I have avoided the temptation to read its history as a
history of "great men and ideas" and have instead set up the
problematics of writing and rhetoric and their historicity as
themes that recur in new settings throughout this book. My
chief motive in choosing this course has been to avoid the
common teleological view of the history of formal rhetoric,
one in which writing is a villain that progressively dismantles,
and then must correct, a lost halcyon day of community and
theoretical unity.

The themes at hand are, then, manifold. They include
the discrete nature of the act of writing and a theoretical view
of this act in the person of a "writer," philosophical positions
that permit (and deny) the imagined "seriousness" with which
we may take acts of writing and their textual forms, traditions
in textual studies that either gingerly or directly counter oral
rhetorical studies, and the way that historical rhetoric has
shaped, and has been shaped by, each of these problematics.
Each of these themes is treated in chapter 1, which establishes
a discrete theoretical background for written composition from
those fields—philosophy, literary studies, and historical oral
rhetoric—that surround it. This theoretical background points
to the great difficulty in denying that writing constructs a
subject quite different from the unitary speaking subject
whom both modern philosophy and oral rhetoric have imagined. From the standpoint of where composition is now and
how it came to be there, we see that our postmodern conditions, those that are described and defined by writing and
written texts, require us to reevaluate our notions of what
writers are, in the broadest senses, "about."

Technologies of writing have produced a writing subject who can, by virtue of its openly provisional claims on
representation, fictionalize the imagined (but always absent)
stability that defines images of the speaking subject in rhetoric
and in traditional philosophy. At the end of this first chapter,

I propose the shape of a textual rhetoric that would address
questions about *writing* in ways that extending the root metaphors of formal oral rhetoric into analyses and pedagogies of
writing are unable to accomplish because they misguide us
about the possibility of direct communication in written language. This textual rhetoric is meant to apply the theory of
the discrete writing subject described early on, allowing its
new view of what writers do to mediate between current
knowledge in philosophy and in literary criticism and the
practical demands of equipping students to enter a written
world.

[handwritten margin notes: question classical rhetoric and the root metaphor while to w redefines the metaphor]

 The strands of interest that come up in this first chapter
have interacted throughout the discourse history begun when
the first inscription of alphabetic writing occurred. But that
history has been told with the situation of the speaking subject, not variable possibilities for writing and its unstable
"presence," at its center. When we instead foreground these
possibilities, as chapter 2 does, we can distinguish a number
of literacies that have accrued with new uses for writing made
possible by its changing technologies. If we place writing and
writers in the center of discourse history from the invention
of the alphabet through the Renaissance creation of the possibility of a purely "written authorship" (a concept that earlier
would have suggested a contradiction in terms), we see that
the field of composition can and should address the writer's
possible identities with a historically informed description of
how technologies of writing and their human instruments
actually interact. The historical description in this second
chapter grounds this study's claim to uncover discourse history that is discretely relevant to composition, for it allows us
to address philosophy, formal rhetoric, and American discourse education with a sense of how technologies of writing
have affected all three.

[handwritten margin notes: foregrounds writing NOT speaking]

 The next three chapters of this book take up these three
areas, raising the thematic issues already described in terms
of each setting. Plato's dialogues, the *Gorgias* and *Phaedrus*,
are treated in chapter 3 as philosophical place markers. They
draw an initial boundary where, for the first time in discourse-
related philosophy, an attempt was made to deal with writing
both as a technology and as a possible site for constructing a

human subjectivity whose 'truth' would always remain in question. Chapter 4 takes up the history of movements in rhetorical studies with the intention of pointing out that actual writing, not a progress of disciplinary "thought," has modified and redefined rhetoric even within its own, decidedly oral, domain. Placing writing in the center of this history suggests some hitherto overlooked interpretations of formal rhetoric's history: Augustine's revisionist rhetoric, for instance, over-turned the Ciceronian "good man" in favor of the credibility of the Christian "Word," which could be divorced from its human source and given credibility through the sermonic "text." And elocution, which for decades has been an embar-rassment both to rhetoricians and to historians of composition, begins to acquire an easily explained importance when it is placed against the growing eighteenth- and nineteenth-cen-tury possibilities that words that had never been *heard* would have to be *read* to revive their formerly assumed human "voices."

These suggestions and others that can be discovered by rereading rhetorical history in light of writing indicate that composition historians, with their discrete concern about writ-ing and its possibilities in mind, might extend my introductory rereading. Similarly, when American discourse education in elitist and then egalitarian rhetorics is reviewed in light of writing, as it is briefly in chapter 5, we see that the "writer" theorized in chapter 1 is also a currently universal "student writer" that composition research and pedagogy continue to describe. The alienation from the written world that the stu-dent must overcome recapitulates all the problematics of the speaking-versus-writing subject, of philosophical history in regard to writing, and of changing rhetorical theories that this book attempts to combine in a new grounding for composition theory and practice.

I realize that the scope of this work may, at least in the view of some, already doom it to charges of superficiality. I have cast this book as a "critical introduction" because its writing pointedly required me to reintroduce myself to texts and to ways of thinking that were, I had thought, "already treated" elsewhere. But as I have tried to rethink what I know of historical rhetoric, the history of literacy and of literacy studies, and of philosophical theory in light of the situation of the student writers whom composition studies takes as a model for study, I have realized how unusual it is to allow actual writing to be a "fixed foot" that gives stability to diverse movements in its related fields of study. Much that is presented here has been "covered" elsewhere, but much that is uncovered here remains hidden in studies based on two assumptions I object to. The first is that the history of discourse has been an attenuation of the primacy of speech situations and a demoralization of univocalic "good men" whose idealized identities we should recuperate. The second is that any field's history may be presented as a history of its "mind," untainted by changing actual conditions around its object of concern. Both views are overturned here to point out that composition studies must take its fully historicized and thus theorized place among prior, but now not precedent, discourse fields.

Certainly this book cooperates with similar projects in composition, especially those that emphasize how written worlds take over the language and intentions of student writers who struggle to use and are simultaneously used by conventions that map textual spheres. But I am extending perceptions of the emergent quality of student writing, like Mina Shaughnessy's in *Error and Expectations* and David Bartholomae's eloquent description in "Inventing the University,"[2] to all writing. Our pedagogical province actually grounds theories of "textuality," the recursive interplay among groups of texts, and the striated and multi-vocal, not "individual," source of written meaning, both of which are common concepts in contemporary theory. These concepts are in no way theoretical for our students, who are (always) learning the conventions of documentation or partially imitating a language that "sounds like" a voice they may have heard or a text they have read, and that they should adopt and be adopted by. Nonetheless, invention in its modern sense is evident in their acts as writers, where it becomes an ongoing struggle either of improvisation against recitation or of "personal" ideas against commonplaces whose trite forms are new discoveries for them. The space in which this tension occurs is a distinct construction by writing, which mediates between fluidity and stability by creating a provisional fiction of "the writer," who is in any form also a "student" making only tentative assertions.

While this point has been made in many other places, it has not yet been fully claimed as the explanation of a historical and distinctly written "presence" that could ground theory and practice in composition studies in a new way. I hope that the restatement and renovation I provide will assert that composition studies must use a fully theorized *writing* to clarify its complex relation to historical rhetorics and to rhetorical practices over time, and that it will allow composition studies to take a clearer intellectual place among analogous contemporary fields.

1 Contemporary Configurations of Writing

Textual Rhetoric

Researchers and teachers with interests in contemporary writers tend to assume that these writers' activities begin in motives quite similar to those that stimulated traditional oral rhetorical events. We generally accept that a writer's activities may have, at least as an immediate outcome of writing processes, much the same result as speech. We make these assumptions on excellent grounds: Oral traditions persist, as do their important influences on written traditions and on particular texts. And more important, we retain a continuing common *perception* of writing as a "medium" roughly equivalent to the speech, and to the text, which many authors and many readers think of as a projection of an author's voice. Consequently, we turn—not only in academic projects but in ordinary talk about discourse—to an established oral model to explain all discourse events. We use the lineaments of a rhetoric based on the primacy of immediate spoken and heard traditions, relying on its foundations to describe how writing, in its broadest sense, works.

This model appears to be sufficient for explaining the generation and features of individual texts as well as their relations to each other. I will argue later that writing has actually, over time, become the unacknowledged foundation of theories in many modern oral rhetorics, but it remains attractive to think (as Walter Ong proposes in *Orality and Literacy*) that we now live in "secondary orality," a literate-oral culture, the eventual outcome of ancient oral-literature culture. Practically, it is certainly true that direct applications of oral models to the teaching and analysis of written texts sustain much research, pedagogy, and writing itself, without much apparent difficulty.

All three of these contextual forces around composition theories and pedagogies have cooperated to help us deny that the writer is distinct from the traditional speaker, a discrete construction from within the actual history of writing that is quite different from the Cartesian, unitary speaking subject whose motives and imagined communicative abilities we continue to relocate at the center of our work. Similarly, these forces and a history of discourse technology that keeps orality and speech at its center have cooperated to help us deny that composition studies is a distinctly postmodern, textual field. But there are problems, both in theory and practice, with either form of denial. All three strands of the braided background we stand within also point toward an inevitable divorce of composition studies from oral models of a single originator of discourse and an orally based belief in the directness of texts. Although theories in literary studies and philosophy have been, as becomes clear, ambivalent about this divorce, exploring this theoretical background and its pointers toward our current position in regard to the writing subject and the possible results of the written text makes it clear that rescuing the fast-declining speaking subject calls for a new rhetorical theory. This is suggested here as a textual rhetoric, a way to account for the variability and even the accidental conditions that actually determine the practical impact (as opposed to the "meaning") of writing.

I am proposing not to solve the dilemma that our history and the shape of current theories place us in, in regard to accepting a new model of a writing subject, but to help us understand the background that encourages, largely on political grounds, the now-outworn retention of the speaking subject even while it offers intellectual alternatives to it. The textual rhetoric at hand is a foundation for a theoretically informed pedagogy that should rest, as the remainder of this book argues, on a history that inevitably led to the distinct writing subject, the writer. Themes in theory, philosophy, and literary criticism point to proposing a new way to rescue this writer, who invites both our theoretical recognition and our applied help in ways that oral rhetoric does not provide.

Nonetheless, neither theoretical traditions nor practical applications of an oral rhetorical model allow us to explain fully the particular phenomenon we have taken to be our object of study, writing. The continuing relationship between writing and speechmaking is volatile, especially in the complicated context of our studies and teaching, where we now find ourselves. This context includes continuing claims on us from oral rhetoric, from philosophical discourses that until recently excluded formal rhetoric because its outcomes are "nonserious," and from common approaches to literary analysis through displaced systematic formal rhetoric.

1   The Writing Subject: A Theoretical View

Those in textual studies with strong conscious and unspoken ties to oral models tend not to conceive of a "writer" differently from the ways they theorize the orator, again for very good reasons. Language that describes the products and processes of the writer and of the oratorical speaker is interchangeable and has been since ancient times. We easily equate the terminologies with writing and speech, whether or not we are aware of theoretical impulsions that impel us to do so. And practically, the two sources of discourse, writer and speaker, both need one or another kind of invention, arrangement, and range of stylistic choice that speech-related categories have given us to use as a way of description. But even work that examines speaking/writing relationships in some detail still leaves the writer as an undertheorized entity in our specialized studies. We rarely acknowledge how writers uniquely mediate between actual and symbolic linguistic domains in ways that place them in a separate and hitherto undescribed textual world.

Contemporary literary and philosophical theories that stem from other interests are surprisingly relevant to the mediation between symbols and actual situations in the practices of writing. Battles between the moderns and the postmoderns have produced distinct technical models for a speaker and a writer that we need to consider, despite their radically limited concern with the situations that actual writers face. Although I am not going to supply what would turn out to be a partial and shallow review of particular theories that take written language as their foundation, which their proponents and detractors have elsewhere made available in detail, these theories are well tested against our work. They can explain a great deal about the action of writing in changing historical circumstances addressed by both "rhetoric" and current "composition."

For instance, explicit descriptions of the speaker and the writer in contemporary theory have been hinted at in the subtle but increasingly clear distinctions between two common ways of teaching writing. Traditional literary freshman English courses are given on a model of "failed authorship," while introductory cross-curricular writing instruction imagines many coequal sources of authority and accomplishment in written discourse. These two easily differentiated practices suggest that we need further articulation of their implied theoretical oppositions, especially in regard to the two sources of origination that they imagine—an implicit model of the speaker and one that accounts for a contemporary writer. Practices we now take to be only parallel versions of writing courses actually inscribe quite different theories of what it means to write, at least when they are explained in terms of new theories and the history of oratory in which special textual concerns arose.

Contemporary theories distinguish among the orator (speaker), the "author," and the writer by pointing out how written words, and by extension the texts they compose, "speak" only among themselves. By this reasoning, texts take significance from local textual receptions, and the meanings of their words from the "difference" among uses of words, not from any positive outside references to actual events or to authorial access to Truth, or to a writer's intentions. In this view, written language is a self-referential or coherent system. It neither depends on, nor results from, vocalizations of "thought." It "operates," with or without our immediate knowledge of its sources and its relevance or reference to anything outside it. It is an ongoing system that actually comes "through," not "from," its instruments, including its writers who may or may not become socially constructed "authors." In this sense, contemporary theorists may say that the person is "written by" language, that is, not in control of it and certainly not its originator.

Many who oppose this reasoning, including traditional rhetoricians who have a great deal at stake in rejecting its reversal of the priority of speech over writing, think that its foundations are in a bad text from Saussure, who grounds this theory in his linguistic description of arbitrary assignments of significance to various sounds. They especially object to its implications for their own theories of "meaning," which they want to attach to the thinking and motives of particular people, both writers and readers, and to explain in further parallel connections between "inside" and "outside" realities. "Inside" and "outside" are also the categories of subjectivity and objectivity that the Cartesian (human) "subject," the originator of language, requires. But derivations from Saussure overcome this dichotomy by placing meaning in language, not prior to it in thought nor in its motivating "situations." This theory thus makes all readings of written language, whether those intended at its inscription or those taken from it, explicitly indeterminate. We are incapable of being absolutely correct or absolutely mistaken as we write or read written language that refers only to itself.

One implication from this theory is that "good men speaking" are neither the sources nor the best interpreters of contemporary textual fates. The range of personal "character" that is now permitted to participate in consequential written discourse has very little to do with the complex effect that a piece of writing may have. As sources, the disenfranchised, the female, even the slave, may "write," without cultural entitlements that are no longer even provisionally guaranteed to anyone. We still in some measure verify our opinions of a text from our knowledge of its writer, but now we most often do this after we know the text, which comes to our attention through institutions and interactions that have little to do with its writer's personal credibility or originating intent. We look to a person who wrote it for confirmation or denial of a response to a text whose "importance" we judge on other grounds.

Similarly, we now have established, even professional-

ized, ways of "reading." But unlike circumstances for evaluation in earlier, predominantly oral settings, our reading strategies do not greatly depend on writers' precedent reputations
or on their personal standing within communities. These strategies do, however, depend on specifically institutional privileges that an age of high literacy began to develop in the
late eighteenth century, as work by textual archaeologists like
Michel Foucault has shown.

I am not about to proclaim the absolute "death" of an
oratorically modeled Cartesian subject, or even of "the author"
who historically re-created the orator's powers, although
those in contemporary theories who see written language as
a closed and self-referential system of signs would assume
that this is a necessity. A differently modeled writer, who is
not the author, has a relation to texts that never exceeds, but
that also must fall within, a greater field of concerns than those
we are accustomed to accounting for in our equations of a
text's possible significance with its "meaning." This overriding
concern, which has long roots wrapped around Platonic realism and extending to formalist literary studies, has it that the
presence of a text depends on its localized meaning, which is
found (or not) apart from the material and social conditions of
textual production and dissemination that actually surround
it. Over time, the author of this meaning has been set aside
in theories that favor its enclosure in the text, and now in the
reader, whose empowerment of a written text is welcomed
even in new theories of rhetoric and composition, which often
equate readers with ancient "audiences" analyzed by Aristotle.[1]

But whatever its source, a basic problem results from
the traditional attachment to meaning, which has its foundations in oral traditions that emphasize the character and intentions of a speaker. This attachment sets aside another proper
theoretical concern in rhetorical studies for contingencies in
discourse production that result from specific circumstances.
This logically important concern requires that "meaning" also
include purposes and actual outcomes from writing, not
merely a mental exchange of "thought" between a text and its
author or its readers. A text that is treated as a static work of
art may logically invite critical positions that focus on authors,

on the marks of writing, or on the reader and "readings," with equally credible philosophical justifications. But the text that we describe in a broader space of personal, historical, political, and social concerns—whether it is a literary or a "rhetorical" piece of writing—takes in a "place" of origin, the descriptive space that only a clear image of the mediating action of a writer can map. In this broader space, an originating presence to a text, the forgotten writer, is more complex than the individual and imaginatively "masculine" subject, whom we conceive of as an independent, potentially totalizing, univocal source of statements. It has been a relief, not just a logical linguistic and theoretical conclusion, to proclaim the recent "death" of that figure.

The writer who enlarges our vision of what it means specifically to explain written discourse lives (as student writers do) in a complex textual world. The writer knows especially about convention, precedents, and "anxieties of influence," the control of already written language over both the meaning and the further actual results of writing. This writer, who is admittedly a fiction whose existence is never called into play outside a theoretically conceived writing event, both originates with, and results from, a written text. As a new version of the traditional subject who was either in control of written language or not, this writer simultaneously sacrifices "meaning" to the resistances of written language, and written language to "meaning," in actual, time-bound performances. And the perduring significance of these performances has little to do with the writer's personal status, his or her intended "meaning," or any other absolutely predictable condition of writing. It is always in question.

This fictionalized "writer," whom I am distinguishing from both "speakers" and "authors," offers us a theoretical basis for a new discussion of the presence of texts in personal, textual, readerly, and broadly "cultural" locales. The writerly subject engages in writing that properly reveals both its "self"-sacrifice and its aggression.[2] That is, this version of the subject performs an assertion by inscribing language, like an actor who concretizes a script when performing in the face of unstable but enabling theatrical conventions. But this writer also defers personal desires and motives in favor of highlighting "the text" that is being performed, but that will be "fixed" only in this performance.

This metaphorical link of acting to writing sheds light on ways that the marks of writing will inevitably be revised and even rewritten once a text is (literally) out of hand. This process will be accomplished even by the writer's own reading of his or her text. Writers will be—are always being—revised, by themselves or by others. Writers therefore embody displacements of meaning, not its stability. Like actors, they claim fixed existence only in grounded and conventional lines on a page. Consequently, writers in the act of writing can be seen as repairing the traditional split between subject and object, making it an irrelevant, if not quaintly false, problem because they are effective only by virtue of their position in an agonistic textual space, where they balance opportunity against constraint.

Textuality, the concatenation of texts that have accumulated and formed discourse communities over time, has provided us with this metaphor of the writing self, who is not predetermined to be either inconsequential or an author. By acting through specifically written language, the writer is always physically constrained; always a conceptualized, rather than completely realized, person; and always consequential or not within specifically textual institutions. It makes sense to acknowledge, in this regard, as Jerome McGann showed in his *Critique of Modern Textual Criticism*, that the actual conditions of writing severely call into question the editorial fiction of the unified, consistent, controlling author. In a primary example, it is clear that for all of William Blake's ability to be a self-contained textual industry, his attempts to author his works outside the total field of concerns that the writing subject accounts for were inconsequential. He could be his own "author, editor, illustrator, publisher, printer, and distributor"[3] but not his own reviewer.

It was not, that is, until strangers intervened in his making of meaning and Blake's work received the insult of mass production that its special individuality could significantly "exist." Blake was not an author so long as his engravings went unsold and unnoticed, although he was attempting to contain all of the elements of authorship as it had been mythologized, from inspiration to final production. But his engravings were made significant when they were "found" by a patron who could get them into the academic discourse that would "appreciate" (use, take life from, critique, interpret, even "require") them. Their "meaning" depends on this contextualization, not on what he, they, or their readers "say."

By saying this I am not, however, fully assenting to a relocation of presence or of authorship in the interpretive field that Michel Foucault described in *The Archaeology of Knowledge* and elsewhere. Foucault's association of discourse and power does provide an escape from the hegemony of the individual text's "meaning" that has marked criticism since the nineteenth century. But empowering—that is, locating presence in—reading conventions and in institutional privileges for one discourse over another does not fully account for the particular version of the active writer that I am proposing.

In "What Is an Author?" Foucault raised, and then dismissed, sociohistorical questions that suggest how we might reconstruct a renovated, written subject. His briefly mentioned concerns show how this concept is as productive and as philosophically reasonable to consider as are the institutions and readers to which he gave priority in the validation of texts. He asserted that his strict examination of the relation between author and text would exclude "how the author was individualized in a culture such as ours; the status we have given the author, for instance, when we began our research into authenticity and attribution; the systems of valorization in which he was included; or the moment when the stories of heroes gave way to an author's biography; the conditions that fostered the formulation of the fundamental critical category of 'the man and his work.' "[4]

Although I am not going to address systematically each of these suggested probes into the history of writing as theorized writers have practiced it, I will take this direction toward specific problems that a history of rhetoric and composition research help to investigate. We know from textual criticism that answering similar questions about "authenticity and attribution" has significant results. For instance, "Wordsworth's" poetry was often the result of collaborations with his sister; Byron revised and sometimes did, sometimes did not, accept his editors' substantive as well as graphic suggestions. We can look for, but not certainly find, textual characteristics to reassure us that what we read was written "by" an individual we attribute it to. Transmitted manuscripts "by" Sir Walter Raleigh and many poets in his time were collected and attributed to these writers after their deaths. Many collections contained variant texts of poems "by" Shakespeare. It is possible that he wrote none of them. But it is also possible to imagine that he wrote all of them, working in an oral-literate manuscript tradition that encouraged improvisation within standard outlines.

The point is that it is not only theoretically questionable but historically implausible to attribute to a written text the power to be a certain pipeline for singular communication, or a wire that carries the voices of the orator or of Socrates talking to Phaedrus. But it is equally implausible to attribute the power of written words only to what amount to accidents of publicity or to readers and their perceptual conventions. Walter Ong has argued that readers are "fictions" within texts, who rise to their newly inscribed identities to respond to the text's expectations.[5] Ong assumes that authors have audiences, that writing is a model of speech. But there are too many holes in a pipeline of written communication to warrant its repair in this manner. Writing is a permeable, discriminatory sieve that needs explanation from more than its fictionalized audience's perspective.

Additional perspectives must, that is, logically account for the prominence of writers over readers, a priority that almost all professional criticism must deny. But the writer's theoretical priority is guaranteed by relative spaciousness. Writers actually and figuratively read *and* write, while readers, in theory and in history, need not. We explain reading to understand writing, the larger category. Writing is not explained to understand reading, unless the tautology of such an explanation is ignored, or both are covertly deferred to a separate entity, the "text."

Once this priority is accepted, we who are interested in both the generation and the analysis of texts benefit from the model of a writer I have outlined, a writer whose texts may or may not become "authored" and significantly "read."

Newly theorized writers who take action in discretely written language are in some measure outside a traditional philosophical hierarchy that places them below a clear and certain relation to truth or puts them in the service of immediate social purposes and their readers. Their mobility in regard to these and other features of the textual situation has everything to do with the limits and capacities of written words, which always contain more than one meaning, and which inevitably inscribe many voices.

This mobility allows a theory of writers to address many questions that otherwise go unanswered: How is the writer we study in composition theoretically possible in regard to the core of self-negation in early rhetoric, with its emphasis on imitation and reiterated commonplaces? How is this writer also possible in relation to the coextensiveness of rhetoric with dominant values in ancient communities? How can the theoretical possibility for individual writing be worked out in regard to postclassical critical emphases on equally self-negating fictions of "genius," "inspiration," and "originality," which tie writers and writing to idealized intellectual contexts as firmly as classical conventions do? How is any writer capable of philosophical "seriousness" in the face of supposed free play among written signs or the persistent distance from intention we must account for in any writing? How can the writer, that is, make a statement when the inevitable juxtapositions of this statement against its many known and unknown allusions will capture and swallow the writer's "voice" and thoughts? And what guides the apparently self-contradictory wish to "make statements" in writing?

A rhetorical view of this writer, and of texts, would answer each of these questions (all of which bring up the capacity of a text to imply presence) by pointing out that writing uniquely mediates between the fluidity and the stability of both interpretations and intentions. Writing, that is, treats the mixed and unstable confluence of anterior intentions and purposes and posterior "readings," "meanings," or outcomes *as though* they could be fixed. It is a living fiction of, not an achievement of, stability. Each text evolves indeterminately and multiply at the same time that it is physically and substantially finished. Every act of writing consequently creates both a preface and a postscript, the writing before a writer becomes a persona and the writing that extends and qualifies its message. Its writer's skill is measured by greater or lesser awareness of how these two glosses on a text itself can engage us.

This is to say that writers are neither entirely independent of nor dependent on systems of language. Their capacity to stabilize fluidity has to do with their abilities to be self-effacing in the service of a conviction that something may be *said* in a particular situation that will be *read* (both by this writer and by some reader) in no particular situation. The writer is self-consciously innocent about "situation" in any case, for situation itself is a fiction, a conventional way to imagine the space of discourse.[6] Again, like an actor whose body mediates a script, which is the "book" of the play in one of its productions, writers re-present presence to us. As any of us knows from experience, they are always deciding to make a statement, within oscillating powers that simultaneously impel and retard the decision.

I have attempted this description because it can renew our theoretical interest in writers who are distinguished from orators and authors. The writer is not an orator whose connections to written meanings or to effects are ideally clear and certain. These writers are also different from the subjects of the composing processes we often describe, for they do not generate, transcribe, and fix meanings independently from the systems of language and cultural history that equally participate in these processes. But descriptions of composing behaviors do in fact support this suggested theory, which makes "recursivity" a feature of the product as well as the process of writing. The primary benefit I seek from this description is that it allows us to renovate the writing subject, whose control of language is admittedly only provisional, but who is not a mere token in a language game. The fundamental risk involved in writing is at issue. The basic result from this risk, the magnificent fiction that writing can stabilize language to give life to marks on a page, is the writer's achievement.

2   A Move to Writing:
Nietzsche on Rhetoric

Although I make no claim to be on the verge of resolving relations between traditional oral rhetoric and all theories of written discourse, the following description of a moment in a very broadly inclusive history of rhetoric does provide a context for suggesting a new rhetorical paradigm that highlights the writer, as well as the implications of writing that I have just described. While outlining traditional rhetoric, Nietzsche suggested problems with it that a new theory of texts might address in its account of writers and the peculiar features of writing situations.

One way to look at definitions of rhetoric from Aristotle on, including Nietzsche's, would be to say that they concern "the art of persuasion" that is studied in a closed and systematic historical and pragmatic discipline. But this art, in its ancient and continuing moments of re-creation, traditionally implied to philosophers who search for determinate Truth an opposition between reductively labeled "seriousness" and "play." As we will see, this opposition is manifest in Plato's *Gorgias;* it is treated there as nutrition versus cookery or medicine versus cosmetology. For Augustine, it was the opposition between God's Word and pagan infidelities like teaching rhetoric. It is a common opposition between theory and practice or between popular and important writing.

Play and seriousness are also prominent terms in specific problematics of writing. In its status as a "medium" rather than a self-contained locus for significance, writing cannot be conceived of as entirely trustworthy. Nietzsche specifically connected rhetoric and writing in this nonserious aspect, thereby opening philosophical discourse to include both, not to dismiss rhetoric and its associations with nonserious uses of language. His lecture notes on rhetoric remain in the tradition of quasi-oral/quasi-written rhetorics like Hugh Blair's published *Lectures,* but they offer distinctly self-conscious philosophical statements about links between rhetoric and writing. The notes place writing and rhetoric together, allowing us to understand their interrelatedness in textual persuasion. Specifically, Nietzsche established a philosophical warrant for the claim that a textual theory separate from oral rhetoric should nonetheless be informed by rhetorical interest in persuasion among situational contingencies, which include the power of writers to fictionalize stability, or "seriousness," in a self-contained linguistic system.

Nietzsche has little credibility as a rhetorical "insider." He was neither a friend to historical rhetoric nor a promoter of its applications, as his undelivered lecture notes make clear. But Nietzsche's notes are an important signal, if not a warning, of circumstances that condition the current *gestalt* or field around "rhetoric." Nietzsche's treatment defined rhetoric as *writing*. It supplied a headwater from which have floated a number of theoretical positions, like those described earlier, about whether it is possible to pin down the truth of a written text's intention, its "systematically" apprehended language, its effects, its interpretations, or its "meaning."

In these notes, headed "Description of ancient rhetoric; lecture—summer, 1874. 3 hours,"[7] Nietzsche immediately drew a line separating his thought from the past. "The concept of rhetoric belongs to the specific differences between the ancients and moderns." Rhetoric is now, he says, in disrepute, and even its best applications are "nothing short of dilettantism and crude empiricism" (99). Nietzsche planned to oppose rhetoric in favor of modern philosophical seriousness:

> Generally speaking, the feeling for what is *true* in itself is much more developed: rhetoric arises among a people who still live in mystic images and who have not yet experienced the unqualified need of historical accuracy: they would rather be persuaded than instructed. In addition, the *need* of men for forensic eloquence must have given rise to the evolution of the liberal art. Thus, it is an essentially *republican* art: one must be accustomed to tolerating the most unusual opinions and points of view and even to take a certain pleasure in their counterplay; one must be able more or less to appreciate the art being applied. The education of the ancient man customarily culminates in rhetoric: it is the highest spiritual activity of the well-educated political man—an odd notion for us! (99)

He quotes Kant as "the clearest" about this: Kant wrote that "rhetoric is the art of transacting a serious business of the understanding *as if it were an amusement. The truth can be articulated neither in a written nor in a rhetorical form*" (my italics). Similarly, describing Aristotle's "philosophical" definition of rhetoric, which has been criticized for its omission of all but the inventive, discovering aspect of rhetoric, Nietzsche again emphasized that substance is tied to thought, not to writing. "Delivery," manifestations of thought, is "incidental" to substance. Nietzsche identifies rhetorical *pithanon*, the intent to persuade, with rhetorical substance. All of the domains of rhetoric are *"already contained"* in it. "This is why every artificial means of the pronunciation is to be made equally *dependent* upon this *pithanon*" (100). Spoken performance, like the staging of a drama, is not necessary to Aristotle's definition.

Nietzsche thus articulates a distinctly postclassical principle that interrelations within modern textuality have further established: rhetoric's five "domains"—invention, arrangement, style, delivery, and memory—are not only an outline of partitioned, linear practices. They also are to be understood simultaneously and interdependently. For example, inventing matter in light of a calculation to persuade would simultaneously determine a stylistic register, so choosing such a register would itself result in discovering the best evidence to support a case. To focus on metaphors, tone, and a calculated voice will result—within that process of focusing itself—in discovering matter, arrangement, and appropriate settings and media for delivery; or, a particular form of discourse (a "book," "poem," "letter") will produce constraints on, as well as developments of, possible content, style, and textual practices that bring an argument to presence.

Relating rhetoric's traditionally discrete domains in this way, as a free play of parts in the intention to persuade, links rhetoric to what Nietzsche called an essentially "amusing" medium, writing. What characterized writing's amusement for him was that writing can merely re-present serious truth. Serious truth is a slower interaction that, unlike writing, does not stand apart from, behind, under, or after actuality. He took Kant's view that "the mythical and the rhetorical are employed when the brevity of time allows for no scientific instruction." Thus writing, which abbreviates both time and space, is like rhetoric. It is playful, not scientific, and is not "about" philosophical 'truth'.

Nietzsche never delivered these lecture notes, although their genre constrained the content, arrangement, and style of the text in which we have them. They were anterior and posterior to an event that never occurred and thus exemplify his view of "writing" as amusement, a play among rhetoric's domains that is not necessarily related to the actual or to Truth. They offer, however, a new philosophical basis for combining textual theory with rhetorical concerns.

An elaboration of Nietzsche's radicalization of rhetoric as writing is Paul deMan's "Rhetoric of Tropes" in *Allegories of Reading*. DeMan, who elsewhere dismissed the "dreary prospects of pragmatic banality" in oral rhetoric as a whole and transitive art of persuasion,[8] nonetheless gives us a way to see the importance of Nietzsche's view of rhetoric as *equal to* written language. Placing rhetoric in a new location, in specifically written discourse, establishes the problematics for a writer that Nietzsche described in his later work. For instance, he wrote:

> It is not difficult to demonstrate that what is called "rhetorical," as devices of a conscious art, is present as a device of unconscious art in language and its development. We can go so far as to say that rhetoric is an extension . . . of the devices embedded in language at the clear light of reason. No such thing as an unrhetorical, "natural" language exists that could be used as a point of reference: language is itself the result of purely rhetorical tricks and devices. . . . Language is rhetoric, for it only intends to convey a *doxa* (opinion), not an *episteme* (truth). . . . Tropes are not something that can be added or subtracted from language at will; they are its truest nature. There is no such thing as a proper meaning that can be communicated only in certain particular cases.[9]

As deMan says, in Nietzsche's view we can see "a full reversal of the established priorities which traditionally root the authority of language in its adequation to an extralinguistic referent or meaning, rather than in the intralinguistic resources of figures" (106). That is, Nietzsche reversed the relation of outside/inside, cause/effect, and especially of language to perception, or "thought." Consciousness, deMan points out, becomes a "linguistic, rhetorical structure" (109). In his view, "the idea of the individualism of the human subject as a privileged viewpoint, is a mere metaphor." This metaphoric construction of a self, which I have placed in the space a theorized writer occupies, substitutes a "human-centered" meaning for the possibility of cosmic insignificance: *"The attributes of centrality and of selfhood are being exchanged in the medium of language. Making the language that denies the self into a center rescues the self linguistically at the same time that it asserts its insignificance, its emptiness as mere figure of speech"* (my italics; 111–12).

Following either Nietzsche or Kant, myth and rhetoric are never philosophically serious, whether they are spoken or written. But to identify rhetoric with writing, as Nietzsche does in quoting Kant and elsewhere, shows not only that Nietzsche knew Plato's views about writing in the *Phaedrus,* but that he saw written discourse as the scene of any nineteenth-century philosophical treatment of rhetoric.

In this new scene, whose emergence traditional nineteenth-century rhetorics acknowledged less radically by drawing analogies between writing and speech, writing in effect replaces the "individual" human subject, who was the previous location of the "intention to persuade" and whose imagined immediate presence determined the effectiveness of persuasion. As deMan points out, this move makes the status of this traditional originating source of philosophical 'truth' moot, for written language itself becomes all that we consider, not the "medium" that conveys intentions and prior realities. Writing becomes the source of significance, the "consciousness" of an interlinguistic, rhetorical structure. In Nietzsche, we find this linguistic source of presence transforming rhetoric from a trivial, primitive, oral art to the philosophical codification, or "language," where presence may be conceived and realized in the reversal of inside/outside, and in the rescue of the self that deMan explains.

By reconceptualizing rhetoric as equivalent to writing, Nietzsche's position allows rhetoric to benefit from, not simply be dismissed by, the historical, philosophical oppositions between seriousness and (written) play whose ancient precedents will be considered in more detail later. But a full realization of this benefit in the form of a new textual rhetoric is also supported by parallel connections between rhetoric and writing outside specifically philosophical writing. The intellectual context established by placing rhetoric within the philosophical discourse that, initially, Nietzsche had excluded has also been established in literary studies. They have gradually, if inadvertently, contributed to making other connections that allow us to reformulate rhetoric in a new theoretical context.

3   Rhetoric in Textual Studies: Background, Text, and Reader

We have a number of institutionalized concepts of writing, as we do of rhetoric. "Writing" may be the privileged postromantic literary work, treated as a stable container for meanings that may be analyzed but not opened to discussion of their cultural purposes or possible alternatives. Such written artifacts are not valued for novel executions of conventional subjects, themes, or techniques, nor for representing community experiences. They have timeless worth because of their imagined technical and lyric (but entirely impersonal) autonomy, endowed by the creation of a textual canon.

More recently, "writing" may also be a self-referential instance of the free play of signs, as we have seen. And on yet another hand, "writing" may be an instance of executing a conventional cultural purpose, with real as well as imagined functions in the service of expression, communication, myth, explanation, documentation, and amusement. In this version, its sources and its effects are related, if not identical, and are thought to derive from techniques and themes that are evocative in a particular community.

These categories are not mutually exclusive or always

rigidly defined in critical practice, for readers' habits are, like those of the audiences for oratory, determined by experience more often than they are by conceptual expectations. But distinct schools of literary criticism do reveal clear precedents for reconceiving "rhetoric" in a specifically textual form.

Historical literary criticism has two ways, one positive and one negative, of preserving and transmitting systematic rhetoric as a context for studying the literary canon. Many historical studies of literary techniques in specific times and in specific works show how a formal, "rhetorical," stylistic system controlled the surfaces of texts. These studies imply that rhetoric was in the life world of the author, part of schooling and imitative practice, an oral residue surrounding the preserved text. Explanations of style are therefore studied *into* the text, where codified system becomes a line between us and the deceased author, not part of the fabric that we, the text, and its author all participate in over discontinuous time. Formal rhetoric, such studies imply, is bottled, canned, and placed on a shelf against a winter of cold explanations. It appears at particularly erudite interpretive feasts.

A related school of historical criticism makes it a point to acknowledge, but finally ignore, rhetoric. It mentions a rhetorical "background" within which a foregrounded literature is thought to have been written and read. C. S. Lewis's statement that "rhetoric is the greatest barrier between us and our ancestors" was not, however, followed by attempting to dismantle the barrier that makes rhetorical interpretations discardable. Lewis hopped over his wall in his description of the nondramatic literature of the sixteenth century, like many others. He used terms that might be applied to literature written by authors and read by audiences whose schooling and sense of convention or propriety had not been based on any of the many sixteenth-century literary rhetorics. As Lewis said, "If ever the passion for formal rhetoric returns, the whole story will have to be rewritten and many judgment may be reversed. In the meantime we must reconcile ourselves to the fact that of the praise and censure which we allot to medieval and Elizabethan poets only the smallest part would have seemed relevant to those poets themselves."[10]

Obviously, Lewis and other students of the sixteenth

century and other "periods" of literature are knowledgeable about pre-Baconian, largely stylistic rhetorics, few of which discussed matters other than *elocutio* before it later became elocution. But allusive treatments like Lewis's are unacknowledged counterparts of the careful preservative scholarship in other historical criticism that does focus on a systematic rhetoric as a background for stylistic choices. Both approaches create a sense that rhetoric, perhaps like midwifery or sumptuary laws constraining the dress of craftsmen, is a curious fact of the past. Rhetoric is not in either view identical with literature, which since the eighteenth century has been read in increasingly narrow aesthetic contexts.

These historical approaches were countered in literary studies by the emergence of the Leavisites and of New Criticism. For most literary analysts since the Second World War, "rhetoric" is an unstable reference to one of two problematic semantic fields. Either it is figurative language—the schemes, tropes, and figures of literary works and controlled style—or it is persuasion—the manipulative scheming of accomplished orators who have become modern "managers" of public opinion.[11]

On the face of it, treating rhetoric as misleading persuasion or "grandiloquent language" appears unrelated to valuing it for providing a catalogue of verbal techniques. But both reductions have resulted from common separations of trustworthy "reality" (equated with content and substance) from "appearances" (equated with untrustworthy outward form). "Substance" is available only as the product of "objective," "scientific," and "impersonal" methods, in whatever age we look for defining standards to certify them. "Form," the ornament and personal style that presents substance, is unreliable and, of course, a way of talking about written language.

Many other sources explain this commonplace philosophical dichotomy. My point here is that it reduces rhetoric in its most comprehensive sense, almost automatically. For example, René Wellek and Austin Warren, whose *Theory of Literature* both announced and recapitulated the foundations of modern systematic English studies, provided a *locus classicus* for modern literary-intellectual positions about rhetoric.

In their project, a specifically literary theory first had to distinguish "literary" from other language, a move that allowed literature to contain substantial metaphoric language that could be taken to be "grandiloquent persuasion" in nonliterary, "rhetorical" discourse. Literary language differs from non-literary language "quantitatively" because rare literary productions have special qualities. "Certain types of poetry will use paradox, ambiguity, the contextual change of meaning, even the irrational association of grammatical categories such as gender or tense, quite deliberately. Poetic language organizes, tightens, the resources of everyday language, and sometimes does even violence to them, in an effort to force us into awareness and attention."[12] After this high evaluation of complex lyric poetry, Wellek and Warren allow that established convention may "poetize" *for* a poet, although "every work of art" evidences unity and organization. In "certain poems," each word crucially constructs the whole.

These values are, of course, now commonplace, in all their elaborations, and they are commonly critiqued by post-formalist and political critics. But neither those who accept them nor those who point out the isolation and separatism for literature that they cause have owned the overt but confused attack on rhetoric—almost an echo of Bacon—that this theorization required. Wellek and Warren found a "much clearer" distinction between literary and everyday language that was actually a waltz around "rhetoric":

> We reject as poetry or label as mere rhetoric everything which persuades us to a definite outward action. Genuine poetry affects us more subtly. Art imposes some kind of framework which takes the statement of the work out of the world of reality. Into our semantic analysis we thus can reintroduce some of the common conceptions of aesthetics: 'disinterested contemplation', 'aesthetic distance', 'framing'. (25)

This pragmatic distinction between art and nonart is, however, "fluid." "Aesthetic functions" may occur in "the non-literary linguistic utterance":

> It would be a narrow conception of literature to exclude all propaganda art or didactic and satirical poetry. We have to recognize transitional forms like the essay, biography, and much rhetorical literature. In different periods of history the

realm of the aesthetic function seems to expand or to contract: the personal letter, at times, was an art form, as was the sermon, while today, in agreement with the contemporary tendency against the confusion of genres, there appears a narrowing of the aesthetic function, a marked stress on purity of art, a reaction against pan-aestheticism and its claims as voiced by the aesthetic of the late nineteenth century. It seems, however, best to consider as literature only works in which the aesthetic function is dominant, while we can recognize that there are aesthetic elements, such as style and composition, in works which have a completely different, non-aesthetic purpose, such as scientific treatises, philosophical dissertations, political pamphlets, sermons. (25)

By the end of this passage, it is hardly surprising to find Wellek and Warren hastening on with: "But the nature of literature emerges most clearly." Before this promise of clarity, they have overtly and implicitly shifted their view of "literary" versus "rhetorical" discourse at least four times. They have used technical rhetorical schemes (paradox, ambiguity, contextual changes of meaning) to define distinctly literary language. They have labeled the persuasive as "mere rhetoric." But they have also reconsidered and allowed literary language to contain, or be contained in, "much rhetorical literature," even treatises and pamphlets. "Style and composition" have become "aesthetic elements," which indeed they are. But reasoning from their purpose, we might have expected their transmogrification into "literary" language to generate new terminology among other new definitions.

Read "closely," this passage is obviously confused and uncertain. It dismisses "mere rhetoric" as persuasion while appropriating figurative language, the only domain of rhetoric studied in literary studies *as* rhetoric for centuries prior. These critics and many others blended grammar into rhetoric, reduced both to "style and composition," assumed that rhetoric is propaganda, and—justifiably in the face of all this—left the literary establishment only with "mere rhetoric."

Theorizing literature into a New Criticism required critics to deal with the problem of how to distinguish literary from nonliterary texts, as it still does. Wellek and Warren were aware that distinguishing literary language from language used to nonaesthetic purposes raised questions about the artfulness of all discourse. Their key strategy was to attribute some of the qualities of literature to rhetorical discourse, thereby revising the traditional trivium, which had equated grammar, dialectic, and rhetoric. Literature became the primary set, the larger entity that includes some rhetorical efforts. This reversal of priorities moved rhetoric from a background in the past to a possible element of a literary text. It permitted the further absorption of rhetoric into "metaphor." "Rhetorical analysis" in literary criticism treats figures of language as a positive, but not as a historical or "actual," force.

Another more recently articulated use of rhetoric to interpret texts also appropriates rhetorical analysis as a positive but not as a historical or authorial force outside the text. Nietzsche's attention to free play in his notes and elsewhere points toward later philosophical programs that guide many contemporary literary theorists following Derrida. These theorists acknowledge that "writing" is a world of its own, a virtuously logical or "cool" space, and a system that signifies the "difference" between one writing and another. In this view, exemplified in Paul deMan's and others' tropological analyses of literature, writing is so far divorced from speaking that a text is no longer imagined to be equivalent to a verbal event or to be the product of an "author." Consequently, while the vehicle of this criticism is "rhetorical" in both specific and general terms, its tenor is antirhetorical. As deMan explained it, this school would omit the "banality" or immediacy of rhetorical persuasion. It places all of the action in literature, the specifically literary language that the earliest New Critics defined to give their work a "scientific" theory.[13]

The avoidance of immediacy that both New Criticism and radical aesthetics insist on results in some measure from formalism, as Jane Tompkins points out in "The Reader in History." As she and others who criticize formalism say, modern literary critics have persistently equated textual presence not with interpersonal and political situations that bring the power of an "author" or of a "writer" to our attention but with the "meaning" whose importance reduces textual situations to mental exchanges between them and their readers. In what I take to be an augmentation of focusing on the distinctness of literary texts, if not on their figural autonomy, the school of reader-response criticism anatomizes these exchanges. Reader-response criticism takes many diverse perspectives on the reader, but if emphases on writer, text, and reader are thought of as sequential points in literary applications of rhetoric, these reader-based critics have further "rhetoricized" the object that semiotic and deconstructive schools "unread" and leave at that.

Susan Suleiman's collection of reader-response criticism, *The Reader in the Text*, exemplifies how this school relocates rhetoric within readers. For her, the word "rhetoric" describes schemes and tropes that are taken to be "rhetoric" in historical preservations. But she also raises issues that are substantially and methodologically rhetorical. Each contributor in her collection proposes to redefine the nature of communication. Each wants to construct a coherent theory that puts the burden of communicative effectiveness not on the author/speaker, nor in the text, but in the reader, who is more than once referred to as the "writer" of any text. More than one of these theorists suggest that a systematic "readatory" could be contrived that would, for some at least, be equivalent in most respects to classical rhetorical codes.

Such codes, as essays in this collection and other similar work claim, would contain the assumed predispositions of any group of readers, including their inclination to dissent about "readings" of the same texts. They would also fit the reading activity imagined by these theorists—a private, individual, at-home activity. Reader-response theory does not assume, as Aristotle did, that there is something called "human nature," or "human understanding"; it explicitly opposes "psychologism," descriptions of ordinary mental/emotional constructs. (Norman Holland, who is represented in Suleiman's collection by "Re-Covering 'The Purloined Letter' " and who receives a number of sharp attacks from other contributors, may differ, but he describes a set of mythic and emotional responses specifically derived from psychology and psychiatry, not from universal "human nature.")[14]

A new readatory would also have to fit the nature of a text that is assumed by reader-response criticism, the privately owned, duplicable document rather than the "public" text that rhetoric in the eighteenth and nineteenth centuries addressed. That earlier vision of the text held it before a community of readers and assumed they could discuss it or might have read it aloud in a group, as George Campbell read his *Philosophy of Rhetoric* aloud to the members of the Philosophical Society of Aberdeen, the friends he had written it for.[15] Assumptions about texts in these literary critical and theoretical programs also lead to objections to the idea of readers as "readerships." Suleiman's introduction specifically objects to a group reader. The text is not an object to be "held," right readings cannot be "scientifically" proved from outside, "meanings" are not stable over time in groups, and texts are not "sent" or "received" in the simplistic communicative model of writing as a channel for anterior thought.

Roland Barthes, in *S/Z*, significantly represents this position: "In the old rhetoric, the choice of *exempla* and demonstrative premises constituted a vast department: *inventio*. Similarly, the classic author becomes a performer at the moment he evidences his poser of *conducing* meaning. . . . Indeed, it is the direction of meaning which determines the two major management functions of the classic text: the *author* is always supposed to go from signified to signifier, from content to form, from idea to text, from passion to expression; and, in contrast, the *critic* goes in the other direction, works back from signifiers to signified."[16] In this view, texts have various "rhetorical" readers, responsive to their placement in what Barthes called semiotic and structural, subjective and psychoanalytic, sociological and historical, and hermeneutic codes. These systems may be either positive (seeking one destruction of meaning) or negative (seeking one stable, decidable meaning).

Reader-response criticism obviously reforms rhetoric in ways that we spot immediately. But this kind of criticism relocates rhetoric entirely within the world of texts, where the motions of "narratees" and critically inscribed readers never become actions in lived experience or textual history. Context (sociology and history), author (subjective and psychological), text (signs and structures), and audience are the issues addressed by this school, but all four are deferred to hermeneutic interpretations, the special code that Barthes called "the Voice of Truth" (21). Barthes found the voice of the reader itself in the text, "whereby we see that writing is not the communication of a message which starts from the author and proceeds to the reader; it is specifically the voice of reading itself: *in the text, only the reader speaks*" (151).

Each of these literary appropriations of rhetoric in historical, formalist, and reader-response criticism uses rhetorical theory, but without fully grasping the antirealist philosophical position it takes in regard to meanings. As Gerald Bruns points out in *Inventions*, treatments of rhetoric as a way to analyze textual surfaces set aside the claim that rhetoric and writing share their philosophical primacy of surface. Bruns reminds us that "inner and outer selves are versions rather than images of each other (a condition that contains perhaps the whole meaning of rhetoric; wherein things are outwardly determined rather than inwardly derived.)"[17] For ancient rhetoricians, he notes, unfixing meanings from referents and placing them in a textual system of differences would be an occasion for an inventory of possibilities, not for a celebration of instability with deconstructionists. "Rhetoric, on [sic] this view, would be the art of making sense in the face of (or in virtue of) the contingency of meanings, or their tendency to occupy the versional state" (89). Rhetoric accepts—is devoted to—the possible versions of statements that various situations generate.

Rhetoric, as Bruns describes it, is most closely aligned to more recent views of the text as a political, not simply an aesthetic, force.

> Ask Socrates what justice is and he will require you to give him a definition, and soon the issue will be whether you know what you are talking about. Ask a rhetorician and he will rehearse everything that has been said about it. . . . The rhetorician knows that whatever is said . . . makes sense only in relation to the situation at hand—a situation that is always in danger

of getting out of hand and turning into a different state of affairs. Hence the intricately political nature of rhetoric, which requires the one who speaks to stabilize, not words and things, but the situation in which he finds himself and which he is called upon to take in hand by what he has to say. (100)

Obviously Bruns's view more radically reasserts rhetoric than any of the textual schools that either openly incorporate its terminology and history or displace them into figural language and readers' responses. He argues for the open acceptance of meaning *as* rhetoric (98), an activity of language engaging a situation. Like Kenneth Burke (who is claimed by both literature and rhetoric as an insider) and Frank Lentricchia in *Criticism and Social Change*, Bruns sees the writer as a "protagonist" (25) who determines whether a language situation is "in hand." Lentricchia would additionally have us avoid the trap implicit in reader-response criticism and in radical aesthetics, the trap of believing that history is an imitation of the literary and that there is nothing "outside" the specifically literary text.[18] For Lentricchia, and in other ways for Robert Scholes (in *Textual Power: Literary Theory and Teaching of English*), the original scope of rhetoric and textual analyses have more than theoretical business with each other. As Lentricchia argues, "Literature is inherently nothing; or it is inherently a body of rhetorical strategies waiting to be seized . . . Literature is not Keats. . . . It is power as representation" (157).

Rhetoric thus becomes in a few programs of textual analysis greater than the grammatical, or paradigmatic, "writing" that guides other contemporary literary theory. Its primary convention, the principle forming its own explanations or "versions," is to treat an unstable situation and language as stable, or "written." Rhetoric theorized in this way fictionalizes stability, just as Plato's Socratic dialogues fictionalize, by making textual, Socrates' inevitably immediate teachings. Rhetoric thus becomes for political critics the writing described earlier as the project of "the writer," writing not entirely within the so-called prison house of past writings or of semiotic systems, "intertextuality." Instead, it is always writing-for-the-first-time, writing that is a process liberated from enclosure in either self-referential language or the world of readers. The rhetoric/writing that Bruns and political critics describe does not begin with phonemes and theorize to whole discourses, it begins with the whole to theorize immediacy into stable texts.

4   Textual Rhetoric

I have been establishing a context for a textual theory in a new look at the writer in an act of writing, a philosophical identity between rhetoric and writing and changing uses of rhetorical theory and its traces in the nomenclature of textual studies. Each of these considerations points out the logic of thinking freshly about "rhetoric" in light of developments that only tentatively acknowledge their sources in an enduring historical concern for taking oral situations "in hand."[19] But these considerations, and the proposal for a textual rhetoric that follows, have, so far, not been situated in regard to current composition studies or explained in order to address potential theoretical connections among currently separate textual studies. Obviously, I have been pointing out what appear to be fundamental errors in applying the model of an oratorical speaker to the textual situation and denying the philosophical connection among all textual studies that Nietzsche asserted and that Lewis, Bruns, and recent political critics differently acknowledge. The textual rhetoric that follows can explain some further ramifications of these errors and specific possibilities for correcting them in an historical account of writing.

But it should be clear at the outset that in specific ways the model I am describing comments on research and pedagogy that are based on traditional rhetoric, and that it could address separations among textual studies. The premises for this theoretical proposal are that writing cannot now be imagined only as a "medium" for direct communication from a singular individual, and that it is always the living embodiment of a risk whose description must vary historically, but which is always the province of a textual "actor" taking in hand a language that in fact can only fictionalize such assertive control. These propositions already point toward, and away from, existing approaches to texts. For instance, they critique research and pedagogies that implicitly center on "meaning," at least in limited ways that do not include in that term the prominent or inconsequential fate of the written text, its writer's motives toward the textual world it enters, or its historical precedents. On the other hand, they suggest that conceptions of writing by political critics and by those interested in social process theories of composition are moving toward a full realization of a textual rhetoric, and away from formalist and elitist views of either products or processes specifically related to texts. These premises equally criticize flatly textual "readings" of written language that disclose either literary or graphic "features" without tying them to the action of a writer in a complete matrix of situational constraints and impulsions to enter a field of written discourse. They reject on theoretical grounds the implicitly formalist, New Critical practices in composition that lead us to assign and evaluate texts in relation to their executions of essentialized "thought," feeling, or a controlled, clear "voice."

Most prominently (in concert with Lester Faigley's proposal in "Competing Theories of Process: A Critique and a Proposal"), these premises and their realization in a textual rhetoric insist on historicizing descriptions of writing. This model could direct us to acknowledge each writing event's relation to its writer, place both in changing material and social circumstances for writing, and relate each to broadly generic textual developments they inevitably encounter. It may accomplish these new tasks in light of historical contexts for writers, rhetoric, and social constructions of the student writer that the following chapters outline.

This panhistorical view also suggests that separations among textual studies like those that divide two fields of composition and literature, or those that Stephen North describes among humanistic "scholars" and empiricist "researchers" in composition in *The Making of Knowledge in Composition*, are probably not logical, but political, differences. Political differences will not be overcome by a new theory that proposes to explain textual generation and reception in a metatheory, for separations arise from historical and social circumstances that cannot be resolved or dismissed in this way. Differing "methods" among fields have material social sources that the textual rhetoric I am proposing could in fact acknowledge. It would be possible, for instance, for each textual scholar and researcher in composition to explain his or her work as an example of explaining a part of the whole model I will outline. But doing so would not overcome the actual bases for separation in research communities housed in nonsymbolic domains. Similarly, opposition between literary and composition studies might be partially overcome by acknowledging that both fields developed historically to deal with the transition from oral to written models in a newly textual world. Literary systems based on classical language study and early rhetorics and neoclassical transmutations of oral rhetoric into composition have gradually made the text and its reader primary concerns, not incidental outcomes from "communication" of ideas or "thought." But a reconceived rhetoric, which provides a way to join these evolving concerns intellectually in a historical progress, does not address the situations in institutional history that have guided the formation of their discrete academic communities.

Nonetheless, my proposal and the historical explanation in the following chapters may make their own difference, especially in the field of composition, by offering historical and theoretical legitimizations that make composition studies parallel to surrounding fields. Composition studies need not rely on the authority of an unchanging, unified oral rhetorical model whose credibility in literary studies has been assimilated and reversed in the partial ways I described earlier. Instead, the field might acknowledge the point in nineteenth-century social history when new graphic locations for consequential discourse obliquely warranted the earliest (and unfortunately continuing) composition courses that emphasized mechanical details, and which further led to the reformations of these courses that composition research now supports.

But none of these possibilities may be realized unless we also acknowledge that oral rhetoric has become in composition studies largely a static, reified totem, the fixed point whose mobile attachments to various subfields of textual studies vary and progress, moving (as Donne imagined) farther from and nearer to them, in unspoken trust. Our silent, habitual connections to oral rhetoric cause us conflicts as well as overly simple resolutions, as the issue of "convention" in discourse can demonstrate.

As either the transmission of ideas or an imitative execution of argument and style, "conventionality" has become a paradoxical concept in a world of texts. Both theory and our own experience of textual worlds make it clear that writers are simultaneously always derivative and always original. Insofar as they are mobile inhabitants of isolated pockets of reading and writing experience, who may unconsciously or consciously oppose comprehensive cultural values and traditional sources for them, originality is their only possibility. But insofar as they also know that writing takes place within a texture of allusions and customs whose sources may be unknown and whose original local communities are now scattered and preserved only in texts, they can only be conventional. Consequently, transferring resources in the "community" that oral rhetoric hypothesizes to resources for contemporary writers and readers is highly problematic. A writer may be learning anew, writing "always for the first time," while a reader may assume that this writing is a cliché. Or, to up the ante even further, the reader may not know the conventionality that the writer intended at all and therefore may take a writer's intended allusion to be a novel locution.

As in many other cases, the actual conditions for contemporary reading and writing cannot be explained by oral rhetorical assumptions. Even traditions that address individuals who act autonomously in well-defined communities cannot be applied to models for writing situations. But neither can we entirely abandon the situational emphases of rhetoric that Bruns explained. Without the persuasive spirit of rhetorical programs, which emphasize bringing reasoning and affective experience into presence to shape a specific setting, we cannot fully understand the dynamics of textual events.

These dynamics are entirely tied to conditions for writing that original rhetoric does not clarify, even by analogy. As the issue of conventionality indicates, writers and readers must often fictionalize each other in ignorance, writing and reading documents qua documents, without reference to a particular "audience." Texts that are not records of what has been said, will be said, or might be said on particular public occasions must take their images of readers, and of "authorship," from projected, rather than personal, qualities. Their writers cannot, in fact, even rely on a shared body of readings that will endow their texts with credibility, as medieval writers might, because reading habits are now fluid and disorganized. Consequently, the writer cannot stop with fictionalizing an "audience," as Ong has suggested, but must also provide signs of how a reader might join the idealized textual space that a particular piece of writing inhabits.

It is tempting to say, as many have, that these signs of participation might be explained by the now-diminished domains of rhetorical "memory" and "delivery," the two parts of early rhetoric that it has been common to ignore since the invention of print. But this sort of comparison is finally too disheartening to pursue because oral rhetoric provided neither for the same citation and documentation we need to establish the identity of a community of texts and readers nor, especially, for the results of publishing, printing, distributing, and preserving written texts. The "non-artistic proofs" described in early rhetoric, which for centuries Aristotle and his followers thought could easily be forged, have become as important to writing as the credibility of its particular human source.

Perhaps they are more important, for witnesses, oaths, and other documentation allow apparent verifiability and "objectivity" in a textual conversation that depends on impersonal exchange. In original rhetoric, neither the errors in writing nor its correctness as a text were issues that affected the credibility of a spoken message. But these simple facts of the text itself are entirely relevant to its endurance, which cannot at all rely on memory in the ancient sense. An extension or analogy from oral rhetoric to written discourse cannot account for the ways that a text will participate in its own continuity after its moment of inscription in a particular situation or for how it may participate in its distribution or impact.

To address the actual practices of those who must write texts, we consequently need to move, not restore, the space of discourse that a comprehensive textual system can describe. It is reasonable to assume, on the basis of the evidence I have already presented, that a textual rhetoric exists already as an unarticulated system in textual studies. Bringing this system to light permits us to retrieve the integrity of oral rhetoric, allowing it to be more than a transmuted system we must make allowances for, a set of *symbols for* the answers to questions about writing. More important, few analyses of texts now conceive of a historically situated writer, who must be simultaneously private and independent while remaining subject to transmission as a public fiction of a person. A textual rhetoric might suggest ways to deal with the text as the product of this writer's action, without fixing the person who writes in one identity that implies writing is now a medium facilitating our contact with the writer's singular thought. The possibility of this identity is attractive but, finally, only an implausible construction around the multiple sources of presence for a text.

Work now on the margins of both oral rhetoric and textual studies can usefully overturn rhetoric, making it a textual study that acknowledges in its title the situational emphases that actual conditions for writing encompass. Language ethnographers, linguists, and philosophers have focused on the following issues that this new model attempts to include in its image of a writing event.[20]

1. *The nature of a written text.* This "nature" includes not only the graphic representation of its words but the complexly determined status of a text as a functionally or aesthetically interesting product. It consequently takes in formalist issues in both composition and literary studies. A text may or may not appear to fix a stable "meaning," and it may record a prior action in a human process. In either of these modes, which are not mutually exclusive, the nature of a particular text also includes its physical form, plausible situations for its reading, and its broadly conceived "place" of origin.

2. *The relation of individual texts, in all of the aspects described above, to the complex, highly textured series of writings that any new act of writing joins.* This series, "intertextuality," includes accruing interrelations among texts that are traditionally explained by a "history of thought." But this series must also include a history of technologies for writing and written discourse conventions. These interrelations have been partially addressed in studies of both literary and rhetorical history, but their fuller description depends on addressing the broad field around discourse that includes changing social, material, and technological circumstances.

 3. *The relation that an individual writer and a particular text take to intertextuality.* This relationship includes ways that the history and conventions of writing surround this writer, who also transforms them in a writing event. Individual acts of writing transcend, modify, or ignore textuality, and these instances are defined by the relation between the writer, the text, and textuality. Developmental studies of individual writers and biographies of authors address this relationship, but they have rarely included the educational, social, economic, and broadly cultural situation of a writer as fundamental issues.

 4. *The relation between the public impact of writing and the individual writer.* This relationship includes all of the issues addressed in current "process" research in composition, but it places individual writing processes against the ways that texts sustain and form cultures and communities. Textual rhetoric requires that situational and historical variations in individual writing processes be recognized in relation to the place a text takes in the history of writing.

This list of issues is still tied to oral rhetoric insofar as it is predisposed to explain writers rather than either "language" or readers. It is also tied to oral rhetoric insofar as it is comprehensive, not limited to one or another feature of a text or of its contexts. The list amounts to saying that the textual world implies all of the consequence and urgency of the sphere of oral rhetoric, and that the tensions between a transmitted code and a particular situational immediacy are transferred to this world.

But this list also ends where predominantly oral rhetoric might begin. The public weal or "culture" that was created and controlled by good men speaking out has not been very important in textual studies. Writing is now thought to be "used" in a broader "communication," or it is treated as a record of "speech actions," but these uses are marginal in textual studies. Textual rhetoric therefore reverses oral rhetoric to place "the public" within the written world, and distinguishes that world from others. Consequently, its primary issue is comprehensively defining a text, but not in the artificially closed way that modern textual studies have done so.

When analyzing any discourse event, we commonly

identify particular *contexts, intentions, situations,* and *manifestations* in signs. We idealize and explain particular cultural contexts and intentions, or desired outcomes within them, as well as discourse situations and their results. Some describe the relationship of these elements teleologically (fig. 1), showing that each determines the limits within which the next may occur, or that each limits the possibilities that follow from specifying it.[21] But these strictly hierarchical or causal, top-to-bottom views of how either written or spoken discourse works are incomplete. For instance, a discourse situation may occur, especially in writing an annual, expected text, well before a prior intention to speak. Even so, the speech that results will depend on the cultural context the speakers share. Consequently, these elements of discourse that are typically identified by, or implicitly interesting to, analysts can be described both hierarchically and interactively. For the purposes of studying discourse, they may be thought to be always in relation to each other and only provisionally deterministic. They are at least interrelated.

FIGURE 1
DISCOURSE EVENTS

Context
Intention
Situation
Manifestation

These analytic relations are further specified by figure 2, which names both *cultural context* and *textual context*[22] as the discrete "context" for writing. Both writing and reading require distinct and separate self-consciousness, if not self-reflexiveness. This recognition can be a minimally intrusive break in the flow of events, that stimulates fluent writers to look for paper and pen, or it can be laborious and burdensomely slow hiatuses that prod the semiliterate who must occasionally read or write. Writing requires an active consciousness to divorce it from the flow of everyday events. It stops time. It is set apart from the communal murmur of discourse, if only by virtue of its relatively recent silent visualizations in the form of independent documents that are not thought of as records containing what might be or has been spoken. Consequently, writing evokes its own context or frames of reference. It needs explanation and accounts that show its relation to immediate *and* to textual contexts created by other writing. As Geoffrey Hartman has put it, writing is "qualified by being framed."[23]

While these requirements sometimes apply to analyses of speech, they always apply when writing is at issue, for even in its most casual forms, writing depends on formal schooling. Whether one has learned only to make letters or has a Ph.D. degree in one of the humanities, writing adds to the consciousness of those who write, for they become conscious of writing. Writing depends on both the broad cultural setting and on the textual setting in which it occurs. This is to say that writing is equally related to culture and to the textual frame of reference, or intertextuality. Its technological, formal, schooled origins have created a series of static texts that make it less able than speech to escape the fiction, or genre, of "history."

FIGURE 2
WRITTEN DISCOURSE

Temporal Contexts
Cultural Contexts   History of Texts
Purpose
Situational Context
The Text

There are many who distinguish writing from speech and from other systems of signification by focusing on the situational level in figure 2. They assume that the same discourse purposes may be accomplished by both speech and writing, depending on the relatively primitive/oral and sophisticated/literate developmental level of the person or culture.[24] Exchanged gestures, tones of voice, facial expressions, timing, rules of dialogue, and physical distance from an audience are some of the elements brought into play in studies of the differences between speech and writing.[25] David Olson, for instance, emphasizes that writing represents what is said, while speech expresses what is meant.[26] To speak "I have misplaced my umbrella" may mean "help me look for it," for

instance. To write this same statement can create, as Nietzsche's and Derrida's play on the umbrella show, an entire
philosophical discourse about writing.[27] Writing is text-bound,
not interpretable only through its situations and their participants. Even a casual note is usually folded to enframe it *as* a
note.

Using only situational analyses of writing would imply
that speaking and writing are equal "modes of communication," either transmitters or, in writing, archives for messages.
Viewed this way, speaking and writing distinctly interest
those who study the "text" of either of these discourse practices in relation to the presence of an auditor or of the absent,
fictionalized, evoked, perhaps dead, certainly distant, intended, or accidental reader. This reasoning implies that either
the pen or the mouth "convey," according to situational appropriateness. If you are here, I say it: if not (and if I am one
of the relatively few who can), I write.

Such a situational distinction surely provokes important and justifiable research, and it sustained the conceptual
integrity of classical rhetoric at least through the Middle Ages.
But to distinguish speaking from writing at this level would
return writing to its original purpose, extending the voice.
To make this situational distinction of speech from writing
prevents us from questioning both modes as creators of messages themselves, as different ways of thinking, and as independent cultural realities. Limited (in the diagram, lowered)
views of the difference might accurately predict whether a
person would speak or write. But beginning to analyze writing
at the level of "situation" would not account for cultural and
individual situations and institutions that specifically result
from it nor address how the act of writing has become a
way of thinking that is concomitant to, but different from,
"making (formal) speeches."

Situational distinctions of writing from speaking also
allow "literacy" to be defined only as *functional* literacy, a
cultural tool or skill. When we instead need "textual context"
as well as "cultural context" to understand a text, literacy also
is necessarily a *textual* tool. It is the ability to act within the
world of texts. Not only is writing in this view a way to act
as a citizen, a professional, a worker, or a socially adjusted

individual, it is also a way of acting in the relived, reflective, interior space of textual interactions.

Thinking that this stable textual ambiance can modify as well as be contained by culture is new in relation to the origins of rhetoric. A written text's meaning or implications—both as text and as act—are always larger than its immediate purpose and situation. Written texts have, and create, their own worlds in which their writers and readers may enlarge and interpret cultural contexts. The writer-in-process, as well as the reader, depends on cultural *and* textual histories. These histories are the broadest possible relevant considerations that motivate either a writer or a reader.

A third figure specifies the elements that stimulate and control written discourse studies. This diagram may be used to describe writing events from the writer's point of view. It also provides a picture of ways to analyze a written text.[28] Its upper elements determine constraints and possibilities that follow, while variations in any of the levels modify the possibilities at the same, higher, or lower levels. It is important to notice that such variations break down the model's hierarchical determinism.

This picture of textual rhetoric permits play among the model's elements. For a textual rhetoric to include a full complement of versions of writing—the product fixing a meaning, the free play of writings, and the mediator between cultural and textual histories and living events—it must not only be understood as the tool of canonized works or of mechanical processes. Hierarchical readings of textual rhetoric work against indeterminate and accidental constraints on forming or on understanding a particular writing.

Both static and dynamic readings become clearer in a demonstration. In the cultural context of a contemporary American research university, and in relation to the long, well-documented history of students taking examinations that we could trace to Socrates' students' notes, the purpose of examining students in writing is appropriate. So is a writer's intention to get a high grade in a university course while entering an academic discourse by displaying his or her understanding of how it works. While in the past the same examination question might have called for a standardized response that

FIGURE 3
THE WRITING EVENT
History

Cultural Context
(Specific era, language
community, attitudes, rules,
values)

History of Texts
(Literacy, "history,"
"literature," cultural
documentation in law,
science, belles lettres)

Purpose
(The desired outcome or best-imagined result)

Situational Context

Participants	Setting	Subject
Personae	Scene	Topic
	(Imaginatively	(The particular
	transformed locale)	aspect of the subject
		as well as its
		"treatment")

The Text

Genre
(E.g., letter, drama, prayer)

Form
(Blocks of discourse, propositional structure)

Order of Semantic Constituents

Lexical Choices
(Vocabulary; register)

Grammatical Structure

Graphic Representation
(Typography, media production, text marking)

recorded the truth in an answer, now the best answers may oppose, transform, enlarge, or bring personal relevance to the question. So the student may have to demonstrate both *an answer* and this latter stance toward the question if a complete grasp of this special discourse is to be made clear.

A student (Participant) thus becomes a student examinee (Persona) when a class (Setting) is transformed into an examination room (Scene), and the amount of real time available to write becomes part of the evaluative scene in which the discourse will be read. The student writes about the (Topic) selected in the (Subject) of the course. His or her imaginative ability to personify a professor as the scholar/audience of this writing, an examiner, defines the professor's role as participant. The (Text) produced will meet the generic expectations of any essay examination; it will not, for instance, be a review or a report. Its (Form) will depend on the number and length or relative weight of the questions in the exam and the response strategies they call for in this genre, in this situational context. And these choices will determine choices of the order of the semantic constituents, the appropriate vocabulary and terminology, the necessary grammatical structure, and, finally, the physical representation of the writing—handwriting—in an examination book.

This description shows how context and decisions made at upper levels may determine outcomes below them. But determining how a particular writing works in a hierarchical analysis is incomplete. The writer, lived experience, or a reader transforms the model in each instance a discourse is entered.

Variance depends on the new locus that these transforming elements bring to the foreground. For instance, a student who does not care about grades will experience writing the examination differently. He or she may conceive another persona, perhaps subtly vary the topic to fit scanty preparation, and produce discourse different from any other in a class. In another situation, a writer may focus on the media at hand and, whether consciously or not, use a word processor or tape-recorded dictation to explore the medium. The text produced will have been controlled—not only in matters of elaboration but also in tone, form, and its relation to the history of texts—by the writer's preoccupation with a means of graphic representation. Or a writer most concerned with the form of, say, comparison/contrast will—as thousands of only partially "assigned" composition essays attest—transform significance, voice, and purpose into unrecognizable background considerations.

Similarly, if the time for writing is shortened or expanded, if its stimulus (in this case, the midterm, the final, the doctoral qualifying exam) is varied, if the imagined reader dislikes answers without (or with) cited sources, or if the cultural context were British rather than American, accurately describing either writing or reading the exam answer would change, as would the answer itself.

The example of the examination might be replaced with examples of literary, public, or distinctly private writings. But this sort of writing is apt for consideration here because it can stand in relation to all of the textual features recognized in the disciplines of rhetoric, literature, and composition. Examination answers seem to be the most ephemeral of texts, but in some measure, literary theory and criticism may in time result from considering this sort of writing event. The examination is a piece of writing in self-consciously public space, as Foucault's analysis of it in *Discipline and Punish* showed. Its student writer is required to "speak for" a received and supportable, not a private, view. But the exam is also always a personal event, and its writing and reading are always privately significant. While stable in itself, then, this sort of text is mercurially perceived.

The model's uses are not merely pictures of textual rhetorical pedagogy—guides for *a* writer or *a* reader—for textual rhetoric also provides a way to look at the disciplines *of* textual studies. The activities of these disciplines are also embedded in the textual world of which they produce versions. Any of the discrete items of the model may become the center of attention in a *gestalt* or field of vision. Consequently, to say that a written text embodies its writer's intention, or semantic meaning, only provisionally describes the text. *A* writing is contingent on shifts and reordered priorities that writers and readers consciously or intuitively make.

The figure can also particularize static and dynamic descriptions of reading processes. "Reading," seen as an analytical mode that provides *a* reading or interpretation, or as an individual or as a disciplinary process, depends on all these contextual and textual elements. In the first, product-oriented interpretive sense, *the* ("ideal") reader accounts for a particular text in relation to some or all of the elements named in the figure. Textual editors, historians, theorists, critics, or readers-for-pleasure consider these aspects of the work, either separately or in relation to others above and below them. *The* "reading" is an explanation of these elements of a writing event.

But like writing, reading is also variable and individual. An ill-prepared or faded manuscript's graphic execution, an unfamiliar or archaic vocabulary, or a blurred genre may either prevent a particular reader's understanding or excite the interest of a student of the writing. Whatever the status of the text, its reader may read only for information (the topic, or treatment of a subject), may read for the situation and genre (e.g., the detective story), may read only to edit at the levels of form and below, or may want to discover the significance of a particular text within the history of its textual context. Reading has particular and individually determined purposes, as writing does. Reading, like writing, may accomplish one or another purpose in light of variations in a reader's knowledge and attention. Both thorough analyses of a "work" and individual reading experiences might be described in reference to this textual rhetoric. Seen in light of this matrix, "reading" refers to deciphering and to understanding a text, not to one or the other.

The model's variance and hierarchy allow us to address the issues listed earlier, which have become significant because the complicated progress of texts includes their eventually bracketed study. The writing event, the individual and ideal writer and reader, textuality, and textual culture are equally visible in textual rhetoric. The text's beginnings as a record of thought or speaking are at fantastic distances from questions that writing creates.

This (or any other) textual rhetoric's inarticulate absence in current perspectives on writing is more and less suitable, depending on our point of view. Its articulation has been prevented by the loss of credibility, if not of the uses, of systematic rhetoric in textual studies. Formulations of local sciences of language have prevented acknowledging origins in, or continuity with, ancient rhetoric. But textual rhetoric's articulation has also been forestalled, ironically, by the desire in literary studies to legitimize its theoretical efforts in philosophy, despite its clearer ties to the particularities of rhetoric. Literary studies have been uncomfortable with highlighting the situational origins and status of texts, for to do so appears to relocate texts in fluid oral culture rather than to preserve them for verifiable or at least widely arguable explanations. The irony here is that literature's subject has never been in philosophy's province of truth. Seriousness, since the *Republic*, has not been taken to be its realm.

For both of these reasons, rhetoric has been the unspeakable ground under textual studies and has also been, in defiance of this silence, the authority supporting them. Individual cases about the credibility of personae (e.g., Booth's *Rhetoric of Fiction*), about the relation of setting to this model's "scene" (e.g., Stanley Fish's *Surprised by Sin: The Reader in Paradise Lost*), or about genre (Frye's *Anatomy of Criticism* or Kinneavy's *Theory of Discourse*) can be placed by textual rhetoric. Any study of textual execution (Richard Ohmann on stylistics, Mina Shaughnessy on student errors), of *a* or *the* writer's development in cultural and textual contexts, of the relation of purpose to subject (Marxist or feminist schools), or of graphic representation (e.g., Hinman's *Printing and Proofreading of the First Folio of Shakespeare*) addresses questions that are authorized in textual rhetoric. New Critical "readings," which claim to explain texts inductively, partially enact this textual rhetorical matrix. They apply rules for and assumptions about the significance of situation, genre, form, and purpose.

It is risky to speak the unspeakable—to propose encompassing studies of writing within a new textual rhetoric and further to claim that this proposal might stand in for original rhetoric better than other discourse models that imitate the physical realities of speaker, speech, and gathered audience. Jacobsen's discourse triangle (writer-text-audience) or its modernized variations in communications and semiotics (sender-message-receiver) have served linguistics, recent rhetoric, and composition studies well enough, despite the reassertion in those schemes of distinctly spoken, direct intentions and responses. These models include context, code, and contact, but they imply a deterministic framework within, not around, language. If this textual rhetoric is to replace them after demonstrably mercurial original rhetoric, we should have some evidence of its place in line. It is not enough to point out that this textual rhetorical system is purposeful, situational, and contingent and thus imitative of classical rhetoric, even down to that mercury-like property of insisting on its atoms while refusing a stable geometric shape.

Textual rhetoric follows, but does not merely recast, classical rhetoric. It takes the text that stands in a field of texts as seriously as ancient rhetoric took the immediate situations and occasions of oratory. The writer, unlike the orator, is working privately in the public, publicly in the private, worlds of texts. While classical rhetoric provides only for a single vision of the orator—Cicero's and Quintilian's "good man speaking" in public—textual rhetoric provides for the multiple, democratic (rather than "republican") versions of the writer that are as diverse as the complexity of writing. The individual who masters the textual elements of the model may use them in the service of the higher levels, or not; a writer may remain only functionally literate without becoming literarily or publicly literate. Or the writer may master and attempt to enter higher levels of textual rhetoric, eventually conceiving new purposes, which may become part of textual contexts and perhaps transform cultural contexts. Some writing makes, to borrow loosely from Derrida, *differance*. In a complex moment within discursive practice that is only incompletely described as the result of canon formation, a writer's actions may prove consequential.

But categorically privileging the literary author or studying writers without referring to an individual's relation to a textual context at a particular time forestalls a full understanding of writing. Writing and reading always occur in human as well as historical time. They have lyric dimensions that may be forgotten. Both "writer" and "reader" have accrued implications over time, so their evolution has not developed a new individual or cultural specie but a series of nostalgic innovations. We still record and assert the voice by writing, transmit textual objects in writing, and as well newly deconstruct the implications of record, assertion, and transmission in self-consciousness about processes of writing.

2 Historical Configurations of Writing

The Space before the Reader

After establishing themes around, and prospects for, a distinct subject (and subjectivity) of written composition studies, it becomes both easier and more urgent to imagine the history of discourse with a writer's possible identities in positions of agency. But acknowledging such active, multiple possibilities for the written subject requires, as I have pointed out, that we arbitrarily invert common approaches to a history of discourse that place orality and coherent oral communities in their foreground. Instead, we need to look at changing technologies for writing as prominent forces that motivate us to reconceive composition studies. Writing has not been, as I will continue to emphasize, a handmaiden to vocal utterances or a destructive force that makes direct communication difficult. But its positive historical participation in creating possibilities for achieving the presence of language usually goes unrecognized, at least in histories of rhetoric and, ironically, of composition.

To accomplish this inversion, I have distinguished a variety of "literacies." This variety of definitions of what it has meant "to write" occurs not in teleologic but in accumulated, disjunctive social and technological spaces that were constructed before readers and the professions devoted to texts moved in en masse to claim writing as their province. From the first inscription of language to the Renaissance construction of vernacular "authorship," a transcoding of oratory to local languages that resulted from print, we see established a set of possibilities that proliferate sites for the written subject.

These new possibilities in the texture of actual practices have been mirrored in momentary looks at writing in doctrines of discourse education. There, brief references by "major figures" in discourse history are valuable sources that constitute a largely overlooked, but nonetheless compelling, alternative educational tradition. Such comments allow us to position the textual rhetoric I have described among its actual, but usually suppressed, precedents. They teased out, if gingerly, problems for the writing subject that also appear in philosophical and formal rhetorical stances toward texts that will be described later.

In the period that this chapter addresses, writers may be scribes, compilers, and commentators on others' writing. They may be authors, a construction that Renaissance critical writing and educational practices at least partially accomplished. In any guise, they have always in some measure submitted to the medium they empower, the physically resistant written word.

1 Ancient Primary Literacy: Hand to Mouth

For most of the centuries since the invention of alphabetic writing, those who compose have questioned what the act of writing implies. Plato appropriately chose the myth of the Egyptian god Teuth's invention of writing (a myth whose truth he questioned) to illustrate that writing may be both poison and healer. We justifiably see the invention of the alphabet in ca. 700 B.C. as the beginning of debates about the implications and impact of Western literacy. But Egyptian cuneiform writing had long before centered another intellectual culture. Egyptian scribes were an elite class who, starting in early childhood, submitted to rigorous physical discipline and years of memorizing and copying maxims and sayings. This material situation charged their written meanings with mystery, the quality of "separation anxiety" reiterated in the representation of writing in the later *Gorgias* and *Phaedrus*, as we shall see. The resulting responsibility and power of Egyptian scribes over the future of their culture was acknowledged:

> A man has perished and his corpse has become dust. . . . But writings cause him to be remembered in the mouth of the reciter. More profitable is a book in the house of the builder than chapels in the necropolis. I see no work which can be

compared to the work of a scribe. You should prefer the skill of writing to your mother. It is the highest profession and there is nothing equal to it. If he [the scribe] is still a child he is already being greeted, he is dressed like an adult. Be a scribe that your limbs may be sleek and your hands become soft, that you may go forth in white attire, honour done to you, and that the courtiers may salute you. Put writing in your heart, that you may protect yourself from hard labour of any kind and be a magistrate of high repute. Write with your hand and read with your mouth.[1]

This encouraging (if intimidating) maxim for scribal students suggests by its references to the writing hand and the reading mouth that writing primarily was used to memorialize what would be or had been spoken. But cuneiform was as complex for its readers as for its scribes. This meant, as the maxim shows, that being able to write was so great an achievement that its masters were elite priests of knowledge, the "learned." Their power to write and read separated them from the domestic and vernacular world of oral exchange, from "mother," just as written texts separate their origins from their destiny. Their abilities were necessarily thought of as mysterious.

Later alphabetic writing, as most students of literacy point out, appears far more democratic because it was comparatively simple to master. But its invention hardly diminished the difficulty of writing while the technology for writing required, as it did in the ancient world, at least seven separate tools.[2] Writing in early Greece was largely done by slaves who were trained to transcribe; it was not a social accomplishment. Reading alphabetic writing, on the other hand, which was at first taught to adolescents but soon introduced in primary school along with making letters, was not so technically difficult. Consequently, the fear expressed by Socrates in the *Phaedrus*, that the text might be out of the hands of the one who wrote it and in the mouth of those unable to legitimize it, had more than one source. This fear not only encompassed the difference between writing's permanence and spoken language's momentary heuristic or dialogic nature. The danger of writing was also by implication the actual likelihood that many would read (or misread), but only a few would write.

Alphabetic writing, unlike cuneiform, socially and education-
ally separated those who could read from those who mastered
writing processes. Consequently, while it carried fewer of the
precedent Egyptian scribal mysteries, it nonetheless caused
more interpersonal estrangement than cuneiform had. Because it separated acts of writing from acts of reading, it placed
the creation of texts outside the "literate," and thus set a
precedent for the special (if later inverted) status of the "mak-
ers" of a text.

We can imagine the adaptations of reading and writing
to spoken language and the reverse, but we cannot verify how
the Phoenician alphabet actually influenced discourse in lost
early manuscripts. Two hundred years passed before alphabetic literacy was generally promoted, so we know very little
of alphabetic writing's first uses beyond record-keeping and
transcribing cultural documents. It has been suggested, for
instance, that the earliest surviving "literature"—satire, political verse, Sappho's lyric poetry—may have been written down
because it did not suit easily recalled musical accompaniment.[3]
Whatever the status of this literature, the Greeks' very earliest
accomplishments in "writing" are not documents of literature
but improvements in graphic technology. In the technical
community, agreements were made that standardized associations of sounds with letters, that made letter shapes uniform,
and that conventionalized reading each line from left to right
rather than alternating directions on sequential lines.[4]

But as the alphabet's graphological efficiency was increased, actual writing also became a social and philosophical
issue that we still and again attempt to resolve. The time
between sixth- and fourth-century Greece contained the variety and pace of, perhaps, our last fifty years, and much of the
action, intellectual and technological, had to do with writing.

Eric Havelock's speculations about this period in *Preface
to Plato* and elsewhere and their echoes in other recent work
on the relation of orality to literacy need not be detailed here.
A culture without iterable texts appears to place significance
in people who physically embody iterability (their "singers"),
not in analytic metasystems that classify, define terms, or
recognize "systems." Such a culture also values and makes
a technology of memory within persons. It self-consciously

returns to moments of utterance by imitating or symbolically reenacting the entire *ambiance* surrounding such moments. In such cultures, the exact words spoken are not idealized "things" to be repeated, but the situation of their speaking is. As Parry, Lord, or David Olson have demonstrated, in speech what was meant is what is meant; exact quotations are not an issue in "accurate" transmission.[5] Memory recalls significance rather than signs.

The "writer" in such a world will have some difficulty finding uses for writing or will at least question the uses that do appear. That is, writing will first be analogous to mathematics or geometry as a way to keep track of commercial details that escape memory, especially memory trained to be macro- rather than microscopic.[6] Writing will also be useful for *looking* at concepts, much as word processing is useful today for increasing the mobility of concepts by allowing them to be rapidly moved and juxtaposed against other concepts not present when they were not composed. Writing will be a way to picture the relations among ideas and their parts as well as to move one part or another around. We "synthesize" (bring together) and "analyze" (take apart) in physical space, at least if we are among early synthesizers and analysts like Plato. He compared both his "Ideas" and the elements of physical nature to the alphabet, whose general patterns of letters could be grouped and classified (e.g., in *Cratylus*, *Theaetetus*, *Timaeus*, 48b 56b 57c). We need not write to have an idea, just as we cannot write before we think of the idea of cuneiform or of the alphabet. But when we do write, we can literally see the relation of one idea, or of an alphabetic code, to other ideas. In these senses, the act of writing was initially useful neither as a means of preserving discourse events that trained memory systems could contain nor as a way of thinking about ideas. It was a way to see ideas as "things" and move them about in nonnarrative, atemporal spaces.

In the ample evidence that writing was at its beginning largely a supplement to speaking and that reading was to hearing, we also have evidence of another sort that will be more thoroughly considered later: texts, literacy, and documents only slowly, if inexorably, were to relocate "rhetoric" and Western ideas about significance, authority, and presence in discourse. The earliest rhetorical handbooks, for instance, did not discuss dislocations of speech that writing might cause, even though they had themselves been written. Those by Polus, Licymnius, and Protagorus, whom Socrates criticized in the *Gorgias*, were not discursive "treatments" but lists of the features of systematic rhetoric that could easily be forgotten. These guides catalogued innovative and specialized devices for judicial pleading or the traditional but difficult-to-remember names of schemes and tropes. Such writing supplemented learning directly from spoken precepts and imitation.

As a new way of remembering details and visualizing concepts, written texts at first had little to do with later problems of their iterability and presence. But these problems came up soon enough in questions about what writing and writers could accomplish in this medium. Certainly the *Phaedrus* posed these questions, as we will see. If we select the writer as a locus for understanding these problems, we can see slowly evolving developments like those described in Clanchy's *From Memory to Written Record* and Chaytor's *From Script to Print* quickly rehearsed in ancient Greece. The earliest comments on the possibility for a human presence in writing are brief early ontological representations of later phylogenic developments.

Isocrates on Writing

Searching out and then justifying new uses for writing was one of Isocrates' ("old man eloquent's") projects. A logographer (literally, "speech writer") and later a rhetorician, he founded his own school in about 393 B.C.. Aristotle is said to have been stimulated to refute Isocrates' rhetorical views by writing the now-lost *Gryllus*, his full treatment of rhetoric. Isocrates is remembered in oral rhetorical history for promoting periodic sentences and for proscribing *hiatus* (allowing vowels to end one word and begin the next). He is remembered among humanists for arguing that the well-educated rhetor must know literature, history, and philosophy as well as verbal techniques.[7] But John Milton's description of Isocrates' death, that he was "killed with report," fittingly suggested another way of characterizing him. He left the earliest view we have of the complex, dual possibilities for placing a self in written words.

Isocrates' criticism of other rhetoric schools in the advertisement for his own in "Antiphon" makes it clear that he understood writing as the "craft literacy" of his time. He says that others teach rhetoric "as they would teach the letters of the alphabet" ("Against the Sophists," *Isocrates* 2:9–11).[8] "The art of letters remains fixed and unchanged, so that we continually and invariably use the same letters for the same purposes" (2:11–14). In attacks on philosophy and rival rhetoric schools, he rejected "alphabetic," or paradigmatic, views of what good teaching should accomplish. Philosophy concentrates on logical oppositions and discovering contradictions ("elenctic"); technical rhetoric mechanically teaches lists of formal devices. Isocrates argued against both and in favor of the ideal of appropriateness, which is the conjunction of technique, knowledge, and talent.

Isocrates also attempted to expand on perceived uses for writing, in opposition to conventional preference for oral, musically accompanied performances of poetry. In "Antidosis," he pointed out that many kinds of prose can teach broad themes while giving as much pleasure as poetry. In this lengthy apologetic defense following a lawsuit against him to share some of his alleged hidden wealth, he used samples of his own earlier prose as evidence of his trustworthy ethos. Although Aristotle later argued in the *Rhetoric* that nonartistic proofs—written testimony and witness—are too easily forged to be persuasive, Isocrates implicitly placed his own persuasive presence in such textual form. He quoted himself to show who he was.

Additionally, in the "Encomium of Helen," much like Gorgias's essay on the same unlikely topic, Isocrates wrote at least partially to give his students a lasting written model. Aristotle cited it in the *Rhetoric* (3:14) as an example of how loose introductions to epidectic speeches resemble preludes to flute solos. Isocrates stressed that visualized, written words and their arrangement in clauses should guide composition more than imitations of high-sounding, lofty diction. Richard Jebb credited him with being "the first Greek who gave a really artistic finish to literary rhetorical prose,"[9] which suggests that Jebb thought of him as primarily a writer, not as he is traditionally characterized as one who could not speak well and therefore took up teaching.

By his own account and others', Isocrates was physically too frail, with too weak a voice, for public speaking. He was afraid of crowds; none of his speeches were written for him to deliver. As a logographer, he derived some vicarious political influence from the speeches he wrote, so while he never entered politics, he was prominent in Athens by virtue of his written opinions.

Consequently, he had good reasons to look for new uses for prose and to acknowledge and answer conventional warnings about its weaknesses and dangers. He addressed its problematic relation to human presence more than once. Using the words "speaking" and "writing" interchangeably (as did most of his contemporaries and followers for centuries), he acknowledged the primacy of speech. For instance, in "To Dionysius" (368 B.C.), he apologized for not delivering his words in person so that he could, as a speaker, immediately erase misapprehensions. He said that "men give greater credence to the spoken rather than to the written word, since they listen to the former as practical advice and to the latter as to an artistic composition" (*Isocrates* 3:2–3). He repeated this judgment twenty years later in the "Address to Philip": "And yet I do not fail to realize what a great difference there is in persuasiveness between discourses which are spoken and those which are to be read, and that all men have assumed that the former are delivered on subjects which are important and urgent, while the latter are composed for display and personal gain" (*Isocrates* 1:24–25). The voice and the feelings of a writer, he says, are lost.

But Isocrates also revealed ambivalence toward already written words and their uses. Greek orators conventionally used exact quotations from passages about their current topics, but Isocrates expressed doubt about the practice of quoting himself. He did so, as we saw, in "Antiphon." But he apologized for doing so in "Antidosis" and "Address to Philip," as well as in "Letter to the Children of Jason" (359 B.C.). He took pains to deny that he was displaying himself, using such quoted passages as showmanship. He wanted the force, or meaning, of these words to be felt; he stressed that they were sincerely meant despite their current distance from him. Such words were sent in friendship, allowing him to conserve his time for carefully presenting advice. On the other hand, he claimed, others had borrowed his language so he might "borrow" from himself. And on a third hand, he said in "Evagoras" and in "Antidosis," prose is a lasting memorial as well as a way to verify a writer's true beliefs.

To see the new paradoxes that writing created worked out in this painful self-consciousness is extremely revealing. Within his reversals and waffling, Isocrates' concern was precisely the possibility for human presence in the newly textual word. He doubted whether the marks on parchment scrolls could convey his conviction and persuade readers that they conserved his personal energy in only the *energeia* of his written style. He, a rhetor who did not speak in public, questioned early writing before its cultural and individual internalizations. The special creative emphasis in his school's pedagogy shows him puzzling out the distinction between teaching what we now think of as "writing" and teaching oral composition plus mechanized transcription. He exposed the raw materials of our own later questions about whether we can directly write a meaning. His self-consciousness about documenting himself and the frequent self-references in his letters show Isocrates finding the first layer of a foundation for our own ideas of intertextuality, the context in which textual rhetoric has become, finally, a necessity.

But writing itself did not evoke a textual rhetoric nor establish an educational practice that dealt with the separation of the actual student of "composition" from written words, as textual rhetoric can. Writing did not, that is, become the primary educational locus for the student's thought, even in this period of high social literacy.

Writing in Early Education

What we know of Greek literature, libraries, and book selling shows how quickly after Isocrates' death writing became common in Greece. The Museum of Alexandria, founded ca. 295 B.C., focused textual activity much as the British Museum or the Folger does now. The museum collected texts—between 200,000 and 490,000 in the third century. It also established the shape of textual studies. Copying, improving punctuation, accenting for correct interpretation (oral deciphering), and writing commentaries went on regularly. By Plato's time, students had also been taught reading and writing in schools and spent their earliest educational years transcribing, correcting, memorizing, and drawing lessons from literature.

This is not to say, however, that writing became the primary locus for generating thought. Reading meant reading aloud; both Hesiod and Herodotus composed history to be recited, not shelved. Students' elaborate memory work was designed to provide them with a store of "common places" to look for things to say. These maxims and passages from especially successful speeches and well-known literature were hear*say* but not second*hand*. Whether composing by improvisation (a method whose traces we preserve in timed written and oral examinations), by "premeditation" (using memory and planning to prepare what to say), or by writing to prepare a speech, a student conceived a "message" with specific reference to vocalizing it. Students wrote on wax tablets, an omnipresent and continuing metaphor for the mind, whose inscriptions could readily be smoothed out to reuse the wax.

We reasonably look at this Greek juxtaposition of textual fecundity and oral primacy from our own perspective, so we rarely leave the two as they were—side by side, not in competition. For us, literacy and orality are always in *super* and *sub* relations. The oral-memory strain may appear to have been primary and dominant at the time because it came from a preliterate tradition that has disappeared from most Western cultures. Or, in a magnificent act of compartmentalization, we imagine and document a continuous *literary* tradition that is "read," as though Sappho, Hesiod, Sophocles, Shakespeare, and Keats could have been engaged in the same creative and specifically textual processes.

Such enframing is the achievement of modern literary criticism, represented in formative treatments like Wimsatt and Brooks's *Literary Criticism: A Short History*. They asserted (in a chapter entitled "The Verbal Medium") that "the important thing about both Aristotle and Isocrates as rhetoricians is, in brief, that they affirm the power of the word."[10] We could investigate the connotation of "word" at length, but it is most clear that "criticism" itself was until the sixteenth century a matter of editing, correcting, and authenticating graphologic transmission of words prepared for speech, not for explaining their independent "power." It was only then that Julius Caesar Scaliger's *Poetics* devoted a chapter to comparing Greek and Roman poets on the same "critical" grounds. Manuscript transmission may have vitalized theological and later textual hermeneutics before this, but there is only a dotted line between the "power" of ancient, primarily oral literary production and Scaliger's work, despite modern literary criticism's telling of the story. As René Wellek pointed out in *Concepts of Criticism*, "a whole volume could be written to explain how criticism emancipated itself from its subordination to grammar and rhetoric, how the word 'criticism' replaced 'poetics' at least in part."[11] This volume would also have to relate each of these considerations to the changing, but for centuries bifurcated and dual, placement of the word's power in either speech *or* writing.

Reviewing what we know of early Greek and Roman education in this dualistic textual world further clarifies the issues that Isocrates raised about the possibility for presence in a written text. The two cultures developed educational systems that were remarkably alike, except that Roman scholars brought their slaves, called "pedagogues," along to school. These companions modified (without entirely changing) the tradition of having a "literate" underclass who only knew writing as a technical craft. Grammar schools taught reading, writing, and—in the service of acquiring commonplaces and moral lessons—literature. Rhetoric was taught to adolescents in private rhetoric schools whose proprietors criticized grammarians for poaching in their province. Plato, for instance, thought rhetorical instruction should be postponed until full manhood; the art of oratory had been at first, as its judicial and governmental uses warranted, adult education.

Courses of study in grammar through secondary schools and later have been well documented. At seven, a child began by memorizing the shapes and names of letters, the sounds of syllables, and next the pronunciation of words and sentences. Students copied and memorized poetry and maxims, much as early American students used spellers to learn letters and wisdom for the purpose of reading, not for writing.

When the child could read and copy, he left the *grammatistes* for the *grammatikos*, who taught basic language and literature. This study, so far as we know, had six parts: 1) reading (practice in prosody; words, at least in Greek texts, were not separated); 2) exegesis of poetic tropes; 3) glosses of rare words and historic allusions; 4) etymology; 5) practice in inflection (reading would be reading aloud); and 6) judgment. The students worked like fourfold exegetes, learning words and grammar as ends in themselves.

At this level the grammarian often introduced the first of rigidly ordered rhetorical exercises, the *progymnasmata*, and later the rhetorician often reviewed and reinforced the grammarian's exercises. These exercises were the fable, narrative, *chria* (amplification), maxim (also amplified), confirmation and refutation, commonplace, encomium, comparison, character sketch, description, philosophical thesis, and discussion of a law. The rhetoric school continued this progress, teaching rhetorical composition as the *Ad Herennium*, Cicero, and Quintilian's *Institutes* portray that study of invention, arrangement, and style. In Rome, declamation was included in rhetorical education; there has been speculation that it replaced the actual occasions for oratory that democratic Greece had provided. Students had "recitals" at which they spoke extemporaneously on assigned topics to invited or drop-in guests. In rhetoric school, they composed compositions that they read to the teacher for correction and comment before they were memorized (and their slates wiped clean). Students did keep notebooks—the commonplace books that survived and flourished again later, when writing replaced memory as a source for imitation at least through eighteenth-century education.[12]

The point of this brief summary is that what was learned about writing was largely *only* about it. Students did not aim for original or personal written compositions, which would have been thought to reveal failures of memory. If we vividly imagine the rarity of textual scrolls as against the plenty of wax tablets, we can easily see that the sparse education in writing, the norm until quite recently, was for representing words intended for oral performance and recitation. This educational system served the purposes for writing of extending the voice and recording thoughts; it supplemented orality even as it quietly fostered an ancient textuality. If we restate the earliest educational practices in modern terms, they become an upside-down form of current priorities in *written* composition. The particular kind of writing ability fostered in the sequence I have described does not teach "writing" as an active rhetorical act but as an ancillary scribal skill.

Anyone proposing these ancient priorities in today's curriculum would meet both protests and a cooperative, if unconscious, nostalgia for this sequence, which implies that "composition" may be learned at one stage of language education that eventually culminates with the good man who "speaks" for himself. These protests are implicit in current textual pedagogies, which encourage students in some instances to write their own stories before they can read others', and which strongly prefer models that begin with the naturalized effects of complex literacy, as textual rhetoric does. Education now adapts learned languages and formalized patterns of thinking like those that were the substance of ancient education to a world of "secondary orality" that these languages and patterns have created. Writing has become a way of thinking, not just a way to preserve thinking for speech. Its instruction begins, fosters, and continues individual development in either localized and private or diverse academic and public spheres.

But were writing still a tool for pronouncing, preserving, and adapting only ancillary texts, "mastering" it before applying it in modern, diverse disciplines (which were once encompassed by rhetoric) would continue to be a reasonable goal. We still in many ways long for this curriculum, as we show in beliefs about what should be learned before secondary or before higher education. The opinion that "reading and writing" can or should be completely mastered before the main business of education begins is an ironic trace from oral curricula that persisted to the end of the eighteenth century and beyond. This belief holds over the oral culture in which higher education taught students to assume public, or precisely rhetorical, voices as the citizen-orators whom Cicero idealized. Insofar as a few institutions educate the elite who will transform cultural and textual contexts (one thinks of Oxford and Cambridge), such expectations would be reasonable still. But in general, we no longer expect education to create "public man."[13]

Many are nostalgic for this recently lost oral culture, whose center was imagined to be the best possible ethos of generalized "human" (male, ethnocentric) nature. In this culture, hierarchical step-by-step learning made sense. Thus, our natural inclination to inform contemporary education with this still-active aspect of an oral residue is also an implicit source for laments for what is curiously always thought of as the recently lost excellence of student discourse.[14] But such nostalgia does not in fact acknowledge, much less celebrate, our own currently internalized textual literacy. This literacy must, because of multiplied fields of writing, be relearned in new contexts throughout educational processes and later. We never get "beyond" writing to oratory as the ancients did in their educational sequence, nor can we stabilize writing's conventions and merely reapply school writing in new settings.

It is important to grasp the continuing theoretical and practical impact of the ancient educational assumption that speech is primary and that writing is its supplement. Many practices in writing instruction reaffirm this priority, despite its inadequacies. But in addition, educational practices extended beyond the discourse situations that first called for them give weight on one side of current academic disagreements among those who debate for and against a metaphysics of hierarchy, teleology, and stable, decidable meaning in a text. These contemporary debates, in large measure, test and restate the terms of varying educational practices. On the side of oral dominance, those who fear that a univocal oral presence will be lost if written texts "could mean anything" harken back to Isocrates' fear that written words cannot persuade unless they are a mouthpiece for a particularized, politicized speaker. They fear losing the accountability of actual people to signs that are not taken to be signs *of*, but are instead tokens in self-referential language systems. The writing and reading that supplemented speaking and could be learned once and early did not raise a specter of graphically or textually lost origins. But the writing and reading that now find whatever "presence" they need in moment-to-moment renewals of a contemporary writer's limited and specifically textual presence, his or her fiction of stability created only in the performance of writing, emphatically do.

Quintilian and the Composing Process

The lineaments of ancient "primary" literacy were still clear in the Roman world, despite its even greater claim on social literacy and its greater reliance on documents and correspondence over great distances. Cicero and Quintilian are, however, two significant contributors to an accumulation of precedents pointing to the problematics of the written subject, insofar as their forays into commentary on actual writing show a tentative awareness of the student writer's special predicament. Both rhetoricians hinted at the possibility, however vague its implications, that students might use writing actually to compose, not just to record, "themselves." In *de Oratore*,[15] Cicero affirmed that "the pen is the best and most eminent author and teacher of eloquence"(150) because it slows articulation. Cicero saw writing as an analogue to polished speech: "The actual marshalling and arrangement of words is made perfect in the course of writing" (151). Writing could also, he noted, control speaking:

> He too who approaches oratory by way of long practice in writing, brings this advantage to his task, that even if he is extemporizing, whatever he may say bears a likeness to the written word; and moreover if ever, during a speech, he has introduced a written note, the rest of his discourse, when he turns away from the writing, will proceed in unchanging style. Just as when a boat is moving at high speed, if the crew rest upon their oars, the craft herself still keeps her way and her run . . . so in an unbroken discourse, when written notes are exhausted, the rest of the speech still maintains a like progress, under the impulse given by the similarity and energy of the written word. (152–53)

Writing was capable of determining speech, he said, long

before Saussure theoretically framed the proposition in other terms.

Quintilian relied on Cicero, but he devoted so much more attention to the virtues and difficulties of writing that we find in the *Institutes* a prototype for a contemporary composition lesson, a lost source that points to current psychologies and pedagogies of good writing. After reading, which promotes judicious imitation and supplies knowledge, he ranked writing as the most important internal aid to oratory:

> We must therefore write as much as possible and with the utmost care. For as deep ploughing makes the soil more fertile for the production and support of crops, so, if we improve our minds by something more than mere superficial study, we shall produce a richer growth of knowledge and shall retain it with greater accuracy.[16] It is in writing that eloquence has its roots and foundations, it is writing that provides that holy of holies where the wealth of oratory is stored, and whence it is produced to meet the demands of sudden emergencies. (3:4; bk. 10)

Here and elsewhere, Quintilian never seemed to imagine that writing would remove presence or persuasiveness from a writer's spoken words. Writing would be "superfluous" if "a single syllable" escaped memory before a speech is delivered (2:44; bk. 11). Unlike Cicero, he thought "it is a mistake to permit the student to be prompted or to consult his manuscript, since such practices merely encourage carelessness, and no one will ever realize that he has not got his theme by heart, if he has no fear of forgetting it" (2:45; bk. 11). He does not even credit writing with the preservative power of memory. He agreed with Plato's objection that writing could ruin memory unless the concentration required during writing acted to imprint words on our minds (2:9–10; bk. 11).

Nonetheless, the writer is a composer, if only and understandably a composer of what ancient rhetoric valued, conventional, influentially spoken, public discourse. Quintilian's attention to writing dealt less with the possibility that inscription could convey the writer's full intentions and more with the possibility that the process itself can actually produce those intentions. We should write slowly and "refuse to give a joyful

welcome to every thought the moment that it presents itself"
(3:5; bk. 10), and we must "frequently revise": "For beside the
fact that thus we secure a better connection between what
follows and what precedes, the warmth of thought which has
cooled down while we were writing is revived anew, and
gathers fresh impetus from going over the ground again" (3:6;
bk. 10).

Once these thoughts, both rewarmed and revised, have
been recorded, they become in Quintilian's description a second self, even an opponent. He was explicit about how to deal
with this shadow presence:

> I do not think that those who have acquired a certain power in
> writing should be condemned to the barren pains of false self-
> criticism. . . . There are some who are never satisfied. They
> wish to change everything they have written and to put it in
> other words. . . . Nor is it easy to say which are the most
> serious offenders, those who are satisfied with everything or
> those who are satisfied with nothing that they write. (3:10;
> bk. 10)

As an example, he cited the nephew of Julius Florus,
Secundus, who after three days had not come up with an
assigned exordium. He was sure he would never be able to
succeed at writing. Florus smiled and said, "Do you really
want to speak better than you can? There lies the truth of
the whole matter. We must aim at speaking as well as we can,
but must not try to speak better than our nature will permit"
(3:12–15; bk. 10).

Quintilian elaborated this example, revealing a pre-
scient understanding of the competition between actual and
textual worlds and between "transmitting" and writing subjects. He advised avoiding self- or text-consciousness, warning
against the danger of allowing writing to substitute for the
language action at hand. Do not, he implies, make the self
into a fictionalized text that only by virtue of prideful imagination can be better than our immediate ability to speak.

We should write privately (at night if that does not
reduce sleep too much) rather than out in the woods as some
say, so that we are not ridiculous and self-conscious when we
experience "the gestures which accompany strong feeling,

and sometimes even serve to stimulate the mind: the waving of the hand, the contraction of the brow, the occasional striking of forehead or side" (3:21; bk. 10). Our writing, he says, should be unmediated by anything that prevents it from staying in the flow of diachronic, sociable, oral experience. And this, paradoxically, depends on concentrating in privacy.

Quintilian also recommended putting aside what we write for an interval before correction, which must neither be careless nor overly scrupulous, "like doctors who use the knife even where flesh is perfectly healthy" (4:3; bk. 10). Neither should orators, like Isocrates or Cinna, take ten years over one piece.

It is worthwhile to review this because it is advice not only to an orator but to a *writer*. The problems, dangers, and solutions that Quintilian addressed would not have occurred had writing still been its original pure supplement to orality, a newly useful preservative craft accomplished only by slaves. His comments suggest that a writer's identity transfers to his text, where it becomes potentially his co-respondent. The temptation to write beyond ourselves, for instance, derives from a sense that the text becomes a mind's representation; it might be invested with our personal worth as readily as our speech. Concurrently in this account, reactions to us can become only reactions to our writing. He recommends that we allow time between composing words like "a newborn child" and return to them when they "will have the air of novelty and of being another's handiwork" (4:2; bk. 10). The "I" who wrote becomes "us," through accretions of experience. I come back able to converse with, elaborate, and correct an earlier self whose presence is now in the text; I am "like another." Writing creates and re-creates this earlier me.

Most of this view of writing is commonplace now and has been a subject of self-reflexive writers since Montaigne, so it may appear overly particular to detail it as evident in primary literacy. When we consider, however, that for centuries afterward writing was largely used as a basis for recitation, Quintilian may be credited with extraordinary and unsettling prescience. He, at the least, demonstrates what writing becomes in times of high social literacy, and it is at least implicit in his views that writing could become a paradigm for the diachronic, not the paradigmatic, "self." Primary literacy, writing to re-present the communal public voice, was also by the end of what we think of as the classical era a potential creator of another self, a writer.

2   Textual Literacy: Writing in the Middle Ages

Although the postclassical Middle Ages provided a number of practical distinctions between one and another definition of what it might mean to write, it is clear that "writing" rarely implied what we now think of as authorship until much later. What is interesting, however, is how the medieval progress of textuality itself began to complicate the position of the writer, adding to ancient ideas about a "recorded speaker" the possibility that texts themselves would become the locus of presence in a written world.

Sources for this possibility are evident in the scrupulous distinctions available in the semantic field that commonly surrounded discourse itself. The common word for composing, as Quintilian's *Institutes* demonstrated, was *dictatare*, "to dictate," which could mean to speak words that an amenuensis would transcribe or to compose words to write oneself. Eadmer, surreptitiously "writing" St. Anselm's biography, was asked what he was "composing and copying (*quid distitarem, quid scriptitarem*)."[17] *Scriptitare*, to write, could apply to someone who was not literate (*literatus*). *Literatus* and *clericus* (clerk, clergy) both meant "learned" or "scholarly," although both were easily qualified terms.[18] Neither word necessarily implied knowledge of writing, the art of making letters. Thus, "laymen" might know letters, but a member of the "clergy" could (at least in the opinion of one knight, Philip of Harvength) "read, understand, compose by dictation, make verse and express oneself in the Latin language."[19] John of Salisbury may have said "Rex illitteratus est quasi asinus coronatus," but he seems to have meant that wisdom, not writing, would prevent a king from being a crowned ass. Kings needed to be able to read the Bible but not to write administrative documents. If they took advice from the *literati* (priests), they also stood a chance of being accounted wise even without the ability to read. *Lectio*, which meant ruminating while listening, was not closely associated with interactions with written texts.[20]

In the thirteenth century, St. Bonaventura distinguished four kinds of writers:

> A man might write the works of others, adding and changing nothing, in which case he is simply called a "scribe" (*scriptor*). Another writes the work of others with additions which are not his own; and he is called a compiler (*compilator*). Another writes both others' work and his own, but with others' work in principal place, adding his own for purposes of explanation; and he is called a "commentator" (*commentator*). . . . Another writes both his own work and others' but with his own work in principal place adding others' for purposes of confirmation; and such a man should be called an "athor" (*auctor*).[21]

As John Burrow points out, these discriminations indicate a technology of making. They imply that sources—not transformations by virtue of reception and publicity among future readers—create "authorship." But additionally, the medieval "athor" only places "his own work in principal place." Within this scholastic tradition of transmission, interpreting someone else's words emerged as a new textual location of presence.

Because we have records both of oral literary performances and scholastic texts from the Middle Ages, we are simultaneously much better informed about "authorship" in that period and more likely to confuse an authorized or authenticated text with our own idea of, and doubts about, consistent, purposeful, unified "authors" who convey a personal presence. We may think that the *Logos*, the Word defined as speech and as reason,[22] had moved into textual authorship. But this does not seem to have been the case. At least early medieval writing did not develop Quintilian's suggestion that what we write becomes another self whom we may want to be better, or think could be less, than ourselves. Instead (as Augustine had prescribed) texts became powerfully "present" themselves. Medieval attention to writing centered on how written texts became, if slowly, sources of authority. Isocrates' concerns about the sincerity of written words are still at issue, but the problem is now with the power conveyed in the document, not with the credibility of an absent person.

The status of ancient texts, which were dispersed, lost, or gingerly stored and copied, brings up the problem of the text's power. St. Augustine had, in his new Christian rhetorical manual, transferred reading and writing, as well as rhetoric, into a religious context. But he also asserted that nothing would be lost if he forgot reading and writing, and with them the vainglories of pagan literature.[23] Before printing allowed wide distribution of copies of manuscripts, the preservation of a text had depended on its often accidental geographic location and the physical labor of cloistered monks, sometimes given one book to copy each year. The hardship of preservation was enormous, even after it was eased slightly by adaptations to smaller miniscule handwriting to make copying a relatively quicker task. One quoted twelfth-century account describes what was involved:

> the tools required for preparing the parchment—the knife or razor for scraping it, the pumice for cleaning and smoothing it, and the boar or goat's tooth for polishing the surface to stop the ink running. Then there are the tools for ruling the lines— the stylus, the pencil, the straight ruler, the plumb line, and the awl for pricking holes to mark the beginnings of the lines. Finally there is the writing equipment itself—the quill pens and penknife, the inkhorn, and various colored inks. This description also includes the importance of adequate heat and good light for writing, although the hot coals recommended seem mainly intended for drying the ink on damp days rather than keeping the scribe himself warm. . . .
>
> Oderic Vitalis, the English historian of the Normans, says at the end of one of his books . . . that he is so numbed by the winter cold that he is going to finish his book at this point and will relate what he has omitted when the spring returns.[24]

In whatever ways we now reread literature and rhetoric of the Middle Ages, the "darkness" of which is becoming less and less shadowy, the time between classical social literacy and early humanism in the late fourteenth century revealed many new versions of writers' identities. Scholasticism, for instance, may be credited with visibly articulating the parts of texts and thus with inventing one of the distinguishing features of literate (learned) thinking, the idea that writing must formalize the categories where ideas reside. Erwin Panofsky, in *Gothic Architecture and Scholasticism*, recounted medieval divisions of texts into chapters and later, thirteenth-century, organization of treatises "according to an overall plan *secundum ordinem disciplinae* so that the reader is led, step by step, from one proposition to the other and is always kept informed as to the progress of this process." "Partes" were divided into members, questions, or distinctions, and these into *articuli*. Panofsky points out that such outlining does not mean "the Scholastics thought in more orderly and logical fashion than Plato and Aristotle," but that they "felt compelled to make the orderliness and logic of their thought palpably explicit."[25] He credits them with the "POSTULATE OF CLARIFICATION FOR CLARIFICATION'S SAKE" (35). While Panofsky may or may not be accurate in endowing medieval thought with the qualities of post-eighteenth-century *Gestalt* psychology, he does make a good case for the medieval connection between sensory perception and the organization—now linear, serial, and visible in texts—of ideas. "Indirectly, this preoccupation affected even philosophical and theological literature in that the intellectual articulation of the subject matter implies the acoustic articulation of speech by recurrent phrases, and the visual articulation of the written page by rubrics, numbers, and paragraphs. Directly, it affected all the arts" (38–39).

In addition to "unconditional clarification," scholasticism submitted to a kind of "authority" different from the classical practice of imitation that had preserved traditions in ancient discourse communities. Scholasticism did extend traditional uses of memorized materials for composing, but it also established a distinct authorization in texts, particularly from the master text of God's Word. Scribe, compiler, commentator, and finally "athor" were, that is, possible only in relation to other texts. My own work may be "in principal place," but it must be confirmed by, or be conformable to, the intentions of others' words. Brian Stock has shown how the eleventh-century debator Berengar, arguing about the specific nature of the transformations of bread and wine in the eucharist, was an individual (assertor) who insisted on combining reason with authority in interpretation.[26] Stock gives Berengar major credit for the acceptance of hermeneutics. But he also notes that Bernard, writing in the twelfth century, "is the active subject of the mystical experience, [but] he avoids the responsibility for the subjective aspects of hermeneutics" (415). Stock's point is that mystical religious experience and related poetic, oral experience slowly changed bards and singers into artistic writers, but that any form of scholastic individualism was anchored in the presence credited to a text and to its interpretations, not in singular and original ideas.

The apparent compulsiveness of medieval intellectualism, however debased Francis Bacon later found its reliance on the logical interplays of words, recursively formalized writers' identities, from scribe to "athor." Writers in this time generally were seen to take presence from and return it to the fact of writing itself. For example, a copying scribe might introduce or return perceptible "error" to a text. Once that error was noted and complained of, "correctness" became its oscillating counterpart and texts, or editions, might be categorized as more or less "error free." A compiler or commentator might similarly include or exclude all the "relevant" supplements to the subject, the master text, at hand. Thus, inclusiveness and exclusiveness became, and remain, categories for classifying texts. At the same time, comprehensiveness could become a quality of the composing process in a new way that ancient imitation had not required. In this medieval concept of writing, the distance forward or back that the "athor's" own work stood from confirmations in other transcribed and compiled texts became the quality of "originality." But *origin* meant only "source," not a psychological matrix of independent creativity.

From the "postulate of clarification" to textual authorship is at least a visible story, verifiable in the obvious features of medieval treatises just as it is by the lexical field associated with acts of writing. We can confirm the medieval evolution of textual presence by examining the newfound force of the document qua document. Just as Isocrates and Aristotle had considered writing to be less verifiable and more open to forgery than speech, medieval readers were unlikely to assume that a piece of writing was as trustworthy as a personal interaction. "Bonds" were spoken words; "getting it in writing" was superfluous reassurance. Writing only slowly became standardized enough to convey a text's trustworthiness, and this trustworthiness was taken to be, as it had been earlier, potentially both medicinal and poisonous.

The permanence of the document was again the issue. In an oral culture, useless laws were forgotten. New rules and customs might replace them without fanfare. Socrates' warning that writing would encourage forgetfulness can be welcomed as well as feared; forgetting, like forgiving, heals. But once documents could take on textual presence by virtue of being the newly "authorized" sources of a broad cultural master text, their permanence was not just a monument or memorial to a significant event, feeling, or person. Their power might remain long after the situation for which they were framed had passed. Ironically, while writing should and must inevitably be revised, it cannot be. It holds our words for us, but it also holds us to words, and holds others to them, long after anyone would wish it.

Consequently, writers in this new context of written clarification developed cases of good reasons for assertions or promises. But the persuasiveness of these cases had less to do with the writer's actual status in a community than with the ability of a text to take intertextual responsibility for its words. Such a sense of authorship is perhaps the essence of pedagogies for academic writing, which always attempt to disabuse students of oral standards for the clarity and permanence of their meanings. Academic writing substitutes textual standards that demand that what is meant be clarified for the sake of clarification and be verified by other texts that can stand behind it as the transient student cannot.

As M. T. Clanchy describes the development of these now-academic standards in *From Memory to Written Record*, the medieval document—whether book, contract, charter, or letter—was attended by visible signs, seals, and ceremonial deliveries to establish its credibility.[27] Forgery was a thriving art, so mistrust of writing and of seals and signatures was reasonable. We can imagine, for instance, that a document represented an oath, a promise, or an arrangement such as a sale, which a scribe had encoded for someone who could neither write nor read writing, however well he might ruminate while listening. The scribe's faithfulness, the messenger's steadfastness, and the reader's accuracy all had to be signified by the document itself, as did the same accoutrements of a reply if one were appropriate. Consequently, elaborate systems of transmittal were devised to authenticate writing, especially between rulers who both might be illiterate, so that their "words" might arrive with the force of speaking that would make them persuasive. In Athens, one might ask Isocrates literally to "stand behind" his words, knowing he had himself seen to their graphic representation. But Charlemagne's correspondents across Northern Europe never could require Charlemagne to have "written" himself.

Only slowly did dating, notarization, formalized terms of address, and formats become standardized enough to allow for revealing "error" in a text, or for its opposite, placing in a text signs that would evoke implicit memories and trust. Our own separation of form from content, *res* from *verba*, is based on the rise of scientific empiricism, but for medieval correspondents, form verified content, or at least the sincere intention to make a specific statement, in writing. It was not the potential iterability of a signature, for instance, that could call medieval intentions into question as Jacques Derrida called contemporary written communication into question by representing himself forging his own signature. His refutation of Gilbert Austin's belief in reliable speech- (or text-) acts would not have applied.[28] But in the Middle Ages, the reliability of intention was already in question, given the novelty of sign-ing, in appointed places, and verifying an intention to "sign" at all through such formalities.

Medieval rhetoric thus became, in at least some of its manifestations, a rhetoric of forms and formats. It formalized, in grammatically codified visible shape, the necessary separation of a particular person from textual presence. This revision of the ancient assumption of identity between a speaker's and a discourse's value was accomplished by finding means to place rhetorical persuasiveness in the text itself. Medieval rhetoric added to ancient systems its own new generic rules, which were necessary because documents themselves had come to stand in for the people as well as for the Word that they meant to convey. By following articulated patterns for greeting, informing, and taking leave of the now-distant and temporally removed "audience," the letter, sermon, or saint's life acquired typical (typological) forms. These forms, along with the signature, could admit particularized variations. Texts became credentials, as one anonymous guide for letter writers demonstrates:

> If one man is writing to one or several or several to one or several and the writing happens to be among equals, or from inferior to superiors, the names of the recipients should be placed first, in the order of the salutation, in the dative or accusative case with their adjectives. The names of the senders, on the other hand, with their corresponding adjectives, should be placed last, in the nominative case. But if superiors are writing to inferiors, the names of the senders should be placed first so that their rank may be indicated by the sequence of the writing itself.[29]

Similarly, medieval rhetoric guided how to plan a document just as Gothic architecture articulated the building. Geoffrey of Vinsauf uses the conceit of building to describe composing:

> If a man has a house to build, his hand does not rush, hasty, into the very doing: the work is first measured out with his heart's inward plumb line, and the inner man marks out a series of steps beforehand, according to a definite plan; his heart's hand shapes the whole before his body's hand does so, and his building is a plan before it is an actuality.
>
> Poetry herself may see in this analogy what law must be given to poets: let not the hand be in a rush toward the pen, nor the tongue on fire to utter a word; commit not the management of either pen or tongue to the hands of chance, but let prudent thought (preceding action, in order that the work may fare better) suspend the offices of pen and tongue and discuss long with itself about the theme.[30]

It is particularly interesting that this passage was meant to guide prose composition. Geoffrey used this method, for example, to compose the *Poetria Nova* that contains it. The postulate of clarification in this rendering does not echo ancient rhetoric's memory systems nor foreshadow later associations among a free play of imagination or of texts. It explains a precisely medieval process in which materials were gathered, examined, and disposed within newly prescribed textual forms, lines ahead of the writer's pen. Neither a well-stocked memory nor the process of writing is generative in this account, but thinking is. Subject, form, and *articuli* should already be in mind before writing occurs.

When we consider the distance between this perspective and our own view that the process of writing creates meaning as well as words, forms, and new thoughts, we must also consider the hardships of medieval writing. If the ink might freeze in the pen held by fingers numbed with cold, we do better to wait for spring than to claim (with E. M. Forester) that we cannot know what we think before we write it. It was clearly possible to look into one's outline, and write.

But at least in regard to opening a space for individual voices, the Middle Ages must be credited with another major contribution to the connotations surrounding the writing subject. That is, despite *and* because of acquiring a new textual presence, medieval writing permitted our later view that texts are not stand-ins for people but depositories for appropriate personae. The problems that justifiably worried Isocrates were partially resolved by medieval formalism, and not only by its demands for nonnarrative articulations of issues, points, and substantiation. This formalism also created elaborate conventional formats for sermons, letters, and legal documents. These documents began to legitimately stand in for oral voices, who may never be heard and whose possessors may be irrelevant to the text's truth. Formal textual codes both allowed and required writers to separate a personal "self" from unaffected, adopted, rhetorical stances. As we will see later, Augustine's new rhetoric had suggested this possibility, which was actualized materially by texts and their increasing prominence as conveyors of the international corpus of Latin learning and official communications.

This artificial textual self-effacement quickly became a "natural" writing voice. Texts could "speak" to each other, in place of people and over distances of time and space, so writers could take on the authority and authenticity of other texts, not just their own relatively weak or powerful articulateness. If unintentionally, the Middle Ages discouraged personal (polemical) positions insofar as it relocated integrity in accurate preservative transmission. It thereby provided a calm space around a new *authorial* integrity. Current composition theory can now debate about whether to foster students' "personal" voices or to encourage imitation of signals of textual authority in various discourse communities at least partially because medieval writing long ago moved the writer's presence away from personal reputation and toward the text's lonely authority.

3 Secondary Renaissance Literacy: "As an Author, I Take More Liberties"

To place the writer in the Renaissance under this heading, "secondary literacy," of course draws on Walter Ong's ways of categorizing movements in orality. "Secondary orality" describes, he says, "present-day high-technology culture, in which a new orality is sustained by telephone, radio, television, and other electronic devices that depend for their existence and functioning on writing and print. Today, primary oral culture in the strict sense hardly exists, since every culture knows of writing and has some experience of its effects. Still, to varying degrees many cultures and subcultures, even in a high-technology ambiance, preserve much of the mind-set of primary orality."[31] Ong's label for this ambiance implies that writing has now taken a hand in all shaped discourse. Writing has become the prototype for all "media," whether they are face-to-face, cover-to-cover, or screen-to-screen.

"Secondary literacy" is an analogous but reversed set of priorities. It does not sustain orality in a literate world but permits technological literacy in an oral, manuscript culture. It allows literacy to be sustained by oral traditions, not the reverse. The term describes a period chronologically later than primary orality, the recording of the oratorical voice, and later than medieval textual literacy, which endowed power to texts themselves. It was the initial stage of working out the implications of print in the relation of writers to their texts and of endowing these texts with the presence credited to oratorical situations.

This period involves such complex realignments of the phenomenology of discourse that giving it a label may be seen to trivialize it. But this label is meant to suggest the reversal that Renaissance critics and poets slowly worked out, dealing especially with the new possibility in print for iterable voices and the concurrent potential for vast distances between an originator and widely distributed words.

As we know, print created a new emphasis, specifically on vernacular writing, the domestic and relatively local product of national cultures that was to supersede international Latin learning and religious documents. It thereby permitted the oratorical situation of primary literacy to reassert itself, holding out the hope that a local elite might become a group of widely recognized "voices," the conceptualized authors whom we still privilege in literary studies. In this particular period, the late fourteenth through the mid-seventeenth centuries, the reader's endowment of meaning to texts was still in question. Writers were held responsible almost absolutely for re-creating the force of vocal persuasiveness, but now in the medium of writing that might become "published," the product of a machine rather than of strictly of human hands. Objections to this new condition were to follow almost immediately, as we see in Pope's attribution of dullness to hack writers whose work was printed.[32] But before these objections were possible, the power of the specifically written voice required considerations and explanations that established the potential for authorship well before a successful "writer" might be judged more or less worthy of that title.

Medieval textual literacy had emphasized dialogue and debate in the context of the superclarification of texts done for its own sake. Textual transmissions called for and got textual interpretations, exegesis and hermeneutics, which imply that an "athor"'s work might take principal place and thus assume a specifically textual persona. By the time of print and the rediscoveries and translations of classical rhetorical texts, writing was well established on many fronts. It was the scribal servant of speech *and* a separate discourse, with its own ways of signaling its trustworthiness and veracity. It could itself be "logical," by virtue of articulation, clarification, and citation. It could stand alone as writ, laws and charters whose power need not derive from personal memories and community traditions.

The new task for the Renaissance writer was, as numerous sources indicate, retrieving the directness of ancient primary literacy to record a voice into this well-established context of textual independence. Building on two foundations, the relatively innocent view of writing as ancillary to the voice and the high-textual complexity that allowed a specifically written persona, the writer in the Renaissance constructed a new identity in the form of a voice that could be distinctly iterable. Whether writing public discourse that was in any measure polemical or attempting to naturalize a medieval genre like the saint's life into homey autobiography, the writer's presence depended on retrieving the unselfconsciousness of the individual ancient, whose writing had been physically and *literally* offhand. Thus, the term "secondary literacy" also implies that the Renaissance writer was struggling with the independent text while glorying in its new possibilities. The impossible task, as time since has shown, was to achieve a directly available presence by *pretending* that printed, published writing could record a "truth from the heart," as scribal writing had in its limited way.

A commonly cited but unlikely reason for postprint visions of what writers might do is a sudden personal or philosophical conviction of individualism. As Elizabeth Eisenstein hammered home in *The Printing Press as an Agent of Change*, Jacob Burckhardt made an unfortunate choice of words to cap his persistently influential interpretation of the difference between medieval consciousness operating "only through some general category"[33] and the particularly Italian Renaissance that he said "at the close of the thirteenth century, . . . began to swarm with individuality" (81). Eisenstein's careful and particularized study of the revolution caused by print technology fixes on this phrase in order to destroy the sort of narrations that Burckhardt and his many followers indulged in. "An historian who is skilled in exploiting selected sources and painting vivid word pictures with his pen can make almost any region at any time seem to 'swarm with individuals,' " she says.[34] In other words, Burckhardt mistook an apparent effect for a verifiable cause. Although "individual" was a new term in the Renaissance, those writers who first benefited from print were not those who reaped the dubious rewards of the later specified "personality," which was an even later evolutionary development.

But Eisenstein's copious study is valuable more for positive than for negative judgments. Her point throughout is that conclusions about the individualism we associate with "authorship" in art, letters, scientific discovery, adventurous travel, multiplied literary genres, the reading public, politics, or philosophy cannot be drawn without reference to the invention of printing and copperplate engraving. Ignoring the impact of these technologies must certainly distort the sources of new accomplishments that seem to have sprung up so suddenly. We would not have our fiction of the individual self without widely available classical texts, many of which had only recently been rediscovered,[35] but all of which were only newly printed and widely circulated. Nor would we honor explorers if they had not had precise charts, maps, and measurements that engraving made available in precise duplications. The personae discovered in the Renaissance might have remained shrouded in "the veil . . . woven of faith, illusion, and childish prepossession"[36] in which Burckhardt dressed medieval man.

Of course, admitting that constructions like "individualism" *are* only constructions that have been particularly congenial in high-literate culture leaves us open to other equally deterministic explanations of change. If we acknowledge that printing revolutionized all the models for spoken and written interactions, we may begin to explain all evidence about these models technologically. We can assume that technological determinism will be as unsatisfying as its counterpart, purely intellectual history, has become in the long run. If we instead step outside comprehensive abstractions and yet beyond concrete technological determinism, we can infer that writers' identities have since print become persistently and copiously overdetermined.

That is, the particular problem of Renaissance secondary literacy might be described as a subtle shift from *authority* to *authenticity*, a quality that needed locations in multiple generic and situational contexts. First, Renaissance writing had the distinct task of repairing what Eric Auerbach called "the irrevocable cleavage between written Latin and popular tongues."[37] To understand how important this cleavage was in the struggle to establish vernacular authorship, we can consider any of the English Tudor and Stuart literary commentators' views of the literary writing of their time. Thomas Wilson (*The Art of Rhetoric*, 1553), George Gascoigne (*Certain Notes of Instruction Concerning the Making of Verse in English*, 1575), Thomas Nashe ("Preface" to Greene's *Meanphon*, 1589), George Puttenham (*The Art of English Poesy*, 1589), and especially Samuel Daniel (*A Defense of Rime*, 1603) reiterate justifications for writing in English and oppose the "schollers"—"studious persons fashioned and reduced into a method of rules and precepts," according to Puttenham,[38] or "irregular idiot" and "deep-read grammarian," according to Nashe.[39] "Schollers" preserved Latin or "inkhorned" it and other languages into English.

As Sidney made clear in the *Defense of Poesy*, the most influential of these manifestos, Renaissance writers were aware of ancient oral vernacular poetry and its closeness to immediate culture. The voice in that poetry is the independent (as opposed to individual) presence that they wished to reestablish, in iterable writing *and* in English.

Samuel Daniel's plea for English, for instance, refers to the equality of ancient and contemporary experiences:

> Me thinks we should not so soon yeeld our consents captive to the authoritie of Antiquitie unless we saw more reason; all our understandings are not to be built by the square of *Greece* and *Italie*. We are the children of nature as well as they; we are not so placed out of the way of judgment but that the same Sunne of Discretion shineth uppon us; we have our portion of the same virtues as well as of the same vices.[40]

Daniel cites the case of Petrarch's Italian writing, which brought him more "glory and fame" than his Latin writing. Daniel was as aware of this point as any current historian of influences on the English writer after the revival of Greek and the spread of print: "Came that mightie confluence of Learning in these parts which, returning as it were *per postliminium* and heere meeting then with the new invented stamp of printing, spread it selfe indeed in a more universall sort than the world even heeretofore had it" (Smith 2:369). Daniel proposed that the writer expresses the nature of his particular state, not the universe of Latin cross-cultural textuality. Vulgar English, he says, links men in the "plain tract" of "custom and the time." He thanked God for his difference from "Schollers" and praised "plodding on the plaine tract I find beaten by Custome and the Time, contenting me with what I see in use" (Smith 2:374).

Daniel's assertion of the special and preferable qualities of writing in English and its capability for moving immediate oral interactions into the place of "universal" Latin writing was not unopposed. Thomas Campion (*Observations on the Art of English Poesy*, 1602) would have taken the retrievals and new publication of the ancients to have reestablished a literary language, free of the rude rhymes of English. Ancient poetry had been served well enough by syllabic verse, "so [far] abandoning the childish titillation of riming that it was imputed a great error to Ovid for setting forth this one riming verse" (Smith 2:331). Campion also thought "iambic and trochaic feet . . . are oppos'd by nature," and offend hearing: "The eare is a rationall sense and a chiefe judge of proportion" (Smith 2:330).

These positions particularly reveal what was at stake for the identity of the writer in the theoretical controversy that accompanied the print explosion of vernacular literary writing. One issue was universal versus local, or national, "voices"; Latin versus English. From scribe to author, and within the medieval church's textuality, writers of legal documents communicated across geographic boundaries that could largely be discounted. The scope of the textual Latin world carried its values and signs of presence with it, as Western values and customs today accompany the world's economic and scientific language, English. Daniel's argument that the world of writing is not translatable nor capable of being a global paradigm recalls Isocrates' complaints that other rhetoric schools taught only "alphabetic" rhetorical rules. Latin writing clearly was, for all of these Renaissance critics, the paradigm whose rules permit canned expression and the dead voice of authority.

In *Timber: or, Discoveries*, Ben Jonson (citing Bacon) expressed this view, saying that "nothing is more ridiculous

than to make an Author a *Dictator* as the schooles have done
Aristotle."[41] As a pun on the name for an orally composing
dictatare, his remark speaks volumes. An author, at least a
classical Greek or Latin or translated-to-English author, had
usually dictated only to a scribe. But in postprint vernacular
culture, these same authors might become the dictator figure,
representing the grammatical, rigorous rules that govern composing in a situation at hand, the province of rhetoric. *Timber:
or, Discoveries* grapples realistically with this tension between
Latin writing and its dictatorship and English writing from
local situations. It offers the first full-blown treatise about the
new authorship in which he claimed to elevate his plays above
more popular entertainment, to the status of authorized English "works."[42]

Consequently, classical imitation, still praised, practiced, and effective today, was in the Renaissance all of these,
but more problematic. The possibility that an individual's writing could be stolen had not existed long before printing, publishing, and copyright law—the new constraint on the old
habit of copying. In Rome, for instance, "the right to an author's work resided solely in possession of the manuscript
(*solo cedit superficies*: The building goes with the ground)."[43]
But after print established "intellectual property rights,"[44] and
words became fully separable from personal ground, imitation
could constitute theft, in the form of translating, borrowing,
or dislocating a learned subject into a vernacular context. Jonson's *Timber: or, Discoveries* was thought by some (e.g., Swin-
burne) to have been his own work; it was only later fully
recognized that it was imitative, mostly a commonplace book
whose "discovery" was Aristotelian *heuresis*, knowing where
to look.[45]

This confusion about the origins of Jonson's "works"
shows how distinct our modern ideas about imitation are. We
generally assume, despite our qualifications of this assumption from historical research, that anything written outside an
academic context, where sources (authority) will be the basis
for new work, is "original." But Jonson and his immediate
contemporaries proudly represented classical values and classic stories as their own teachings for the unlearned. They
justified any of their deviations from Latin practices, cele-

brated the English language, and stole from each other with great goodwill. The royal tutor, Vives, might say that teachers should be more than "a conduit from ancient authorities."[46] He therefore instructed students in the traditional belief that imitation is assuming the persona, not the words, of another: "To imitate Cicero is to put yourself in Cicero's place. . . . Follow Cicero, therefore, through one of his speeches: take up his theme, and try to work it out in your own way. . . . In this way you become acquainted with Ciceronian rhetoric, not by directly copying him but by entering into his spirit" (200).

But the paradox of imitation became increasingly insupportable under the pressures of authorial writing personalities and impulses to trust the self's observations as well as received wisdom. Jonson, for instance, in his essay on wits, proudly noted that critics can seldom be quite sure that his borrowings are not unconscious recollections from past readings rather than translations from an open book.[47] Thus, while vernacular writing and its implications were newly being celebrated, Renaissance writers also began to perceive magnificent new problems of authority. These writers were at once transmitting, teaching beyond an established curriculum of transmission, and creating new common places for writing in public discourse. Many of the commentators on Renaissance literature list the new genres and new authors in the English vernacular whom they cite for contributing to distinctly English, distinctly written, traditions. Sidney, Spenser, Shakespeare, More, Chaucer, or Donne appear to have been canonized immediately for displacing the old *literati*'s power into this new context of wider literacy.

Daniel's comments also addressed this important relation between a *literati* and an inevitably new potential within literacy. Print created, as early manuscript transmissions had not, imposingly large opportunities for the literate vernacular poet, a new being. We are likely, for instance, to wonder why rhymed versus syllabic poetry was so hotly contested (as Campion's comments on it exemplify) if we ignore a deeper tension between old oral cultural habits in spoken, sung, improvised, formulaic verse and distinctly written poetry. The poet who is writing must convey, whether this writer's poetry is to be recited, read aloud, or read silently, the same hypnotic energy as the singer of tales. Both rhyme, in the primarily stylistic rhetoric dominating the period's handbooks, and iambic (English) meter may restore to the visual medium of print the spoken and heard music of the language. Similarly, metaphors and similes, which often crop up in Renaissance prose as lengthily extended conceits, preserved the narrative story lines that were important in oral literature, but now in scholastically clarified and articulated written oratory.

In Renaissance writing, such devices indicate attempts to endow a text with the oral powers—the presence—of the ancients. If a writer's manuscript is handed along, either by messenger or across the tables of a literary circle, its signs of authenticity reside in it and in its oral reading. But a printed book or a miscellany copied and circulated widely only teasingly asserts an instant "loudness" in a larger group. The author of this sort of text must recuperate gestures, body language, and a powerful voice to it. Rhetoric had always acknowledged the importance of the rhetor's natural talents, but these talents were not just the creative genius discussed in Plato's *Ion*, as Isocrates' comments on writing explained. The Renaissance writer of any sort automatically faced an additional problem beyond his possession of native genius, a problem of assuming a publicized but silent and potentially duplicable voice. Before readerships were wide enough to claim their own styles and to establish professionalized interpretive communities, the stylistics that dominated Renaissance rhetoric was the best refuge for individual power.

We must distinguish this problem from the customs associated with earlier writing. For medieval scribes, compilers, commentators, and even "athors" whose work held one, if principal, place, a single or authentic voice had been only ambivalently sought. When found, it was often excused as the result of mysticism. The universal community of Latin texts heard God, Church, and Prince through a rigorous grammatical formalism that was predetermined and could be more and less "correct." These forms supplied a textual music, if not its words. But writing in the vernacular, particularly in non-Romance English, with its greater distance from classical languages, proposed many new difficulties for establishing presence in writing. Whereas medieval writing sought to empower texts with their own credibility, texts that might be printed to convey an iterable "voice" required additional ways to reestablish an oral community's belief in the human voice behind a specifically written text. This new situation pressured a writer to find ways of "speaking," not merely "saying," written words.

Education in Vernacular Writing

It would be possible, of course, to reason about this issue of new "authorial" writing and its implications for the historical subject from the new audience's, the reader's, perspective. Vernacular printing invited participatory culture. Although those who try to measure the amount of general literacy in the Renaissance are unsure about what percent of men and women in England were able to read or write, signs of a steady increase in reading (before a later decline) are clear. In 1543, for example, the Act for the Advancement of True Religions enjoined a large group of people from Bible reading, although it is likely that Bible listening and ruminating were also intended to be proscribed. Well-founded guesses suggest that literacy may have increased from about 10 percent to about 42 percent among men from 1500 to 1700.[48] We know of about two hundred titles in the *Short Title Catalogue* between 1576 and 1650. But as David Cressy points out in *Literacy and the Social Order*, this number of titles, at fifteen hundred copies from each printing, would have been absorbed easily by the same "gentle, clerical and professional" readers who always constituted a high-literate elite (47). The number of books published and sold discounts the spread of printed ephemera—fly sheets, proclamations, and advertising, whose generality suggests that many could read or would be close to someone who could. Protestantism certainly encouraged reading; *The Office of Christian Parents* (1616), for example, said that illiterate children would become "idle . . . vile and abject persons, liars, thieves, evil beasts, slow bellies and good for nothing."[49]

Whatever the state of general literacy, the idea that common English should be both *langue* and *parole* in Renaissance England, both the paradigm for thought and its local form of utterance, was strongly stated in educational treatises well before Bacon or the Royal Society promoted a plain English style. For instance, a move toward a paradoxically elitist egalitarianism was promoted as early as 1531. Thomas Elyot's careful discrimination of *plebs* from gentlemen in *The Book Named the Governor* prototypically stated the doctrine of degree and its appropriately elite view of who should be educated. But Elyot nonetheless made a point of stressing that plain English writing would be the way to allow *shared* governance among this elite. In the proheme to *Of the Knowledge Which Maketh a Wise Man* (1533), he wrote:

> I intended to augment our Englyshe tongue, wherby men shulde as well expresse more abundantly the thynge that they conceyued in theyr hartis (wherfore language was ordeyned) hauynge wordes apte for the pourpose: as also interpret out of greke, latyn or any other tonge into Englyshe, as sufficiently as out of any one of the said tonges into an other. His grace also perceyued that through out the boke there was no terme new made by me of a latine or freche worde, but it is there declared so playnly by one mene or other to a diligent reader that no sentence is therby made derke or harde to be understade.[50]

Before even an elite class of readers could participate in the new religious, political, and literary worlds that were constructed by vernacular print, English had to be made "literate," as Elyot and others attempted to make it. English must be made a language that could translate received wisdom, *and* become the medium of writing what men "conceive in their hearts." It was not enough to transliterate from Latin to plain English words, as Ralph Lever did (in the *Arte of Reason, rightly termed Witchcraft*, 1573). There "preface" became "forespeach"; "conclusion" was "endsay"; "declarative" and "conditional" became "showsay" and "ifsay."[51]

This and other attempts to domesticate English for English thought are well documented in the critical writings cited earlier and in modern historical commentaries like Richard Foster Jones's *Triumph of the English Language*. When we read the syntax of some of Jones's examples, we see the problem of finding an easy English. These examples remind us of the garbled syntax of students (or ourselves), finding language for new and complex concepts. Jones quotes:

An artificiall Apologie, articulerlye answerynge to the obstreperous Obgannynges of one W. S. Euometyd to the vituperacion of the tryumphant trollynge Thomas Smyth. Repercussed by the rygtht redolent and rotunde rethorician R. Smyth P. with annotacions of the mellifuous and misticall Master Mynterne, marked in the mergent for the enucliacion of certen obscure obelisques, to thende that the imprudent lector shulde not tytubate or hallucinate in the labyrinthes of this lucubratiuncle. (95)

The fragmented syntax of this amusing 1540 introduction is certainly as problematic as its language, which appears to be looking for spelling and persuasive alliteration within its right, redolent rhetoric. Written English may not have become more efficient, or "relatively readable," as E. D. Hirsch claimed in *The Philosophy of Composition*,[52] but it has at least lost such echoes of spoken poesy to favor a standard Subject/Verb/Object and Agent/Action/Goal disposition of its intentions.[53]

As written English vocabulary and syntax slowly became naturalized and literacy concurrently spread, readers of course slowly became accustomed to learning by reading. For instance, the transition from hearing Bible readings and sermons to reading them for oneself was matched by changes in school curricula. And Elyot's *Book of the Governor* is organized by the sequence of readings he planned for students. As in times before and since, many learned to read who could perhaps make letters but not imagine themselves using writing to compose discourse. A new connection between reading and spelling (and the otherwise inexplicably venerated place of correct spelling today as a sign of intelligence and probity) is exemplified in a lesson from Edmund Coote's *English School-Maister* (1596):

JOHN: How write you *people*?
ROBERT: I cannot write.
JOHN: I meane not so, but when I say *write*, I meane spell: for in my meaning they are both one.
ROBERT: Then I answer you, that p,e,o,p,l,e.
JOHN: What use hath (o) for you give it no sound?
ROBERT: True: yet we must write it, because it is one of the sounds we learned, wherein (o) is not pronounced.[54]

This lesson was intended to demonstrate to teachers how

they might teach spelling and reading without actual writing, which could be put off until later, or forever, in the elementary curriculum.

Reading and writing as we conceive them were separated as differing grammar school and secondary or university levels of literacy. Rhetoric was still taught after the basics of literature and language and was the basis for learning to compose one's own discourse. Although schoolchildren did generally learn to make letters, to develop a fine handwriting, to copy, to take dictation, and to imitate those they read, their composition at all levels was as often in Latin as in English. Milton's Latin prolusions (responses to the ancient *progymnasmata* exercises) are prominent examples of the nature of this "original" composition, which was one's own Latin treatment of an ancient topic. Translation from Latin to English and the reverse, which Benjamin Franklin domesticated in a reading-to-writing American version to improve his style, was also typical.

Although some composition of essays and themes was taught, it turned out to be rule-governed composition, a matter of fitting thoughts to prescribed forms that were something like today's five-paragraph themes. The process is exemplified in Ralph Johnson's 1665 *Scholar's Guide* (forty-three pages of "Short, Plain, and Basic Rules for performing all manner of Exercise in the Grammar School").[55] This Strunk and White of the time shows how little connection there was between a reading curriculum and the idea of vernacular written composition. Oratorical ability was still the distinct purpose of higher education, although acquiring this ability increasingly depended on reading ancient models that could be resuscitated, as we shall see later, by studying elocution.

Renaissance practices in vernacular education thereby inadvertently contributed to the possibility for an elitist vernacular authorship. They associated reading with spelling, not with learning to write, a later program embedded in training for imitation that was emphasized in university treatments of rhetoric. It is paradoxical that the availability of printed Bibles and the generally democratic Renaissance tendency to allow children from all classes to attend elementary schools fostered this divorce between those who might eventually compose, and those who would only decipher, written language. In the ancient past, all who began school were already part of the elite who might complete it, so elementary lessons were part of the well-designed staged curriculum that was to develop the citizen-orator. Nonetheless, we find indications in Renaissance educational documents that English language would be composed among a governing elite and only read among the classes who leave school after elementary lessons.

Sidney's Prescient Original: Authorship as "His Own Stuff"

These customary educational separations between those who read, and those who will compose, writing were widened, as we have seen, by new ways to distribute writing in published forms. Yet, some space still remained before the silent and isolated reader could focus a written conversation as one of a "readership," imaginatively placed in a noiseless rhetorical stadium. Writers still had to construct these readerships imaginatively, without the help of well-defined markets or the support of established assumptions about their own credibility. Writers' relations to written words and to the act of composing them were, in this transition, their responsibility, as their statements about fulfilling this responsibility show.

Sir Phillip Sidney's *Apology for Poetry* addressed this question of responsibility, and of power, implied by a new authorship. Sidney's *Defense* was not merely an exercise in opposing Plato's ostracism of poets. It also implicitly answered questions in the *Phaedrus* about how written words may be "heard" at a distance. Sidney was, that is, not only defending poetry's superior representations of reality but laying foundations for the author. He established competition between vernacular poetry, philosophy and history, two discourses that had been recorded since Plato and Herodotus. A philosopher "teacheth, but he teacheth obscurely"[56] "by certain abstract considerations" (25). The historian is tied to the particular, "laden with old mouse-eaten records, authorizing himself (for the most part) upon other histories, whose greatest authorities are built upon the notable foundations of hearsay" (24). The poet, superior to both, "doth draw the mind more effectually than any other" (41).

Without reviewing Sidney's argument about the nature of poetry, we can notice that the main issue in many of the contexts he creates in his discussion of poets is their authority. He acknowledged the easy power of oral singers, bards, and balladiers, whose lyric voices are equated with music and song. He was at pains, however, to praise verse while insisting that verse is not poetry's essence. Thomas More's *Utopia*, for instance, is compared to Virgil's *Aeneid*. What was more centrally at stake for poets appears to be the character and divinity of poetic *making*, which Sidney clearly and repeatedly addressed without reference to the poet's audience.

Sidney's claim is that the poet is the monarch "of all sciences" (38). "Whereas other arts retain themselves within their subject and receive, as it were, their being from it, the poet only bringeth his own stuff" (50). Here expressing the commonplace distinction of poetry, that it comes from poets' own imaginations, Sidney further distinguished the Renaissance writer's new power of assertion: "Neither let this be jestingly conceived, because the works of the one be essential [actual or real—ed. note] the other in imitation or fiction; for any understanding knoweth the skill of the artificer standeth in that *Idea* or fore-conceit of the work, and not in the work itself" (15–16).

This locus for the assertive writer, taken to be an autonomous maker who "to imitate borrows nothing" (20), has been, of course, common in literary views of the writer whom we have imaginatively privileged. But Sidney was only establishing equality for written vernacular literature as against long-transmitted philosophy and history, as well as an equality between written and bardic poetry. In the process, he asserted written literature's superiority by claiming that the writing poet introduces presence to the text in the form of "Idea," the power of independent making.[57]

In *The Shape of Things Known*, Forrest Robinson has associated Renaissance visualization with Sidney's argument, including the visualization of thought allowed by "the Gutenberg Revolution."[58] Robinson also notices the direct connection between Sidney, Fulke Greville ("A Treatise of Human

Learning," 1633), Gabriel Harvey (*Ciceronianus*, 1577), and other anti-Ciceronian Ramists. This school, he claims, was attracted to Ramistic visualization of thought (150–54) and repelled by a rhetoric of words, or of style. But stylistic rhetoric itself had much to do with visible language, as recent prescriptive stylistics based on reading efficiency and the principles of "discourse processing" suggest.[59] Whichever rhetorical school was favored, Ciceronian or Ramian, connections between thought and the articulated, visible page of writing were commonly made. But in Sidney and elsewhere, these connections between thought and visual articulation may be seen to generalize, and by participating in Platonic Christianity to universalize, the poet/writer's thought.

Presence, the issue of the nature of written subjectivity, thus becomes directly related to a text's specifically visual disseminations. The writer, conceived by Sidney to be capable of "making" in a new world of shaped discourse that has been sent off alone but is not yet entirely in the reader's lap, has placed *authenticity* in texts. Sidney and his contemporaries superseded an older medieval textual presence. They made it clear that what was being asserted anew was the maker's power, which retrieves the ancient spoken presence of individual prophecy, divination, and powerfully composed oratory.

To say this is not to deny that Renaissance writers were aware of growing audiences beyond scholarly and literary coteries. Exactly the contrary was true, as the relation of print to reading in participatory culture and to multiplying genres and topics for published writing shows. Sidney and all of his peers note their audience, write prefaces directly to their readers, and take more and less overt trouble with publication and book sales. But the point of their asserting writers' powers in making was in large measure a response to a further development, that culture could in their time be generalized beyond scholasticism.

Nonetheless, in this era that explored the possibilities of English vernacular print and developed so many newly acceptable written genres, we also witness the first written utterances by what might, in deference to Chaim Perelman's "Universal Audience," be called the "Universal Writer." Uni-

versal writers, better known as authors, assumed the preroga-
tives of the ancient orator and poet. They could write in favor
of, or oppose, nationally applicable opinions. They claimed to
"know," by virtue of having touched origins in ancient wisdom, social custom, and religious-philosophical traditions and
having united these sources with distinct origins in themselves—ideas, the fore-conceit. They mediated past against
future interests, whether educational, political, religious, legal, military, or imaginative, and did so without support from
the traditional "rhetorical situation" but with a presumption
of shared insight.

The orator's likeness to the poet as well as to philosophers and historians was often remarked on in the Renaissance, as it had been in ancient sources. As Michael Murrin
points out in *The Veil of Allegory*, Sidney, Webbe, Hoskins,
Puttenham, and other Renaissance *litterateurs* acknowledged,
as Jonson put it, that "the Poet is the neerest Border upon
the Orator."[60] The figures of style are of course common to
both poets and orators. The demand for linguistic perspicuity
that is made in both of their discursive practices requires
clarity for the audience's sake, not the textual clarification
of scholasticism for its own sake. Persuasiveness to moral
action is the duty and privilege of both. Murrin has claimed,
however, that once writers like Jonson burlesqued in fact
and dismissed in spirit the invocation to the muse, "at one
blow they pulled down the temple of allegory" (169), and
with it the rhetorical mode.

From within the borders where literature now stands,
Murrin's conclusion is arguable. From outside, however, Jonson's insistence on writing from his own rather than from
divine powers of observation merely demonstrates continuity
from Sidney and toward the Royal Society or Swift. Allegory
was at the time but one, if the first, of the ways that rhetorical
teachers might teach rhetorical knowledge, at least in the rhetoric of late fourth-century Greece and after. The other means—
"preface" (stating and summarizing the argument's points),
"art" (a running commentary on an argument), "history,"
"figure," and "idea" (the important relation of style to the
whole)—might equally convey the rhetorical mode, even as
later novels ("histories") conveyed it.[61]

Consequently, we need not assess Sidney and his contemporaries by later standards to recognize how they established oratorical presence in writing. They found the ground on which the writers who followed them might diversely mediate community experiences to unknown readers through even colder type. These later writers' responsibility for the presence in their texts increased after direct lines to divine presence were torn by influences from regicide, new priorities for science, and rationalist philosophies. But these writers accepted their roles, writing with unapologetic assurance in any of the new genres encouraged by print. Post-Renaissance writers imply that their books will be taken seriously even beyond direct spatial, temporal, and social connections with their readers. But the burden of this assurance, a new function of print, is evident in their many defensive or credentialing prefaces and their self-deprecating conclusions, earlier conventions that abound throughout seventeenth- and eighteenth-century texts. Nonetheless, the increasing solidity of authorial assertiveness and power is now spread far beyond the elite group Sidney envisioned as its source. It is manifest in the multiply complex literacies that we might catalogue in post-Renaissance writing.

To describe briefly only one example, the growth of this assurance that a printed text will convey authenticity is clear in a progress of authorship in the eighteenth-century English novel. We find Richardson and Fielding still scrupulously explaining that *Clarissa* is a collection of letters and that *Tom Jones* is "told" by a historian who has everything under control, but who cannot be sure of what his actors were thinking and must "read" them from visible clues. But by the time Smollett, Sterne, and later writers make similar claims, we think of such explanations as poses—ways to educate a growing readership. In the short time between the early and the later, more "established" novels, first-person singular writing became able to sustain the credibility of many writers and their readers. Early doubts about veracity and reliable evidence in printed texts became narrative conventions, part of a literary/literate game.

Secondary literacy cannot, however, be reduced to a matter of persona or of authorial stance. What was at issue after the invention of print appears not to have been the ability to tell a story or to incorporate authorities into authorship, at least not on the evidence reviewed here. The issue was rather how ancient and later textual conceptions of presence in a written text might be assimilated by new communities of authors and readers in their vernacular, local situations. Authenticity is not a function of isolated, inward sincerity, for a writer may be apparently or secretly in disagreement with his or her printed words. What is more important than sincerity is the possibility that printed vernacular writing in all its forms convince us that it is a "real presence," what a textually fictionalized person meant to say. Whether the new writer's sources are tradition, custom, patristic and classical received opinion, imitated works, divine creativity, the new Anglican "I," or supposedly "objective" scientific observations, each of these sources must be focused so that writing becomes the automatically chosen way both to make an assertion and, as is inevitable in print, simultaneously to efface the self.

Written texts, having achieved unmediated (textual) rhetorical possibilities, thus developed distinct authentic voices that could compete with local as well as ancient customs, traditions, and wisdom. The intrinsic distance of writing from experience consequently became its particular quality of superiority. We have learned from written texts to value assertions beyond their immediate, original, and verifiable situations. Developments of the new power Sidney imagined for written words are obvious: the entirely written character and self-reflexive and self-discovering authorship.[62] From Sterne to Vonnegut, Wolfe, and Mailer, the written, observable self has flourished in secondary literacy. Its common topics include in later times the alienated, the fragmented, and the unverifiable—as well as the inductive, the experimental, the knowledgeable, the experiential, and the factual. These major accomplishments of our highly literate modern writing have become paradigmatic notions that we are now revaluing: "history" of great men and ideas, "philosophy" as an individual statement rather than a culturally determined representation of reality, "character" as a fixed, essentialist, already written construct, and of course the "text-itself."

Secondary literacy by no means replaced the primary and textual literacies I have described. While it relied on and followed both, all three modes obviously continue. Writing might be said to have developed chronologically, through these sequential relations between "composition" and the status of texts. But writers—at least those who inhabit current "secondary orality"—may not experience ancient writing-to-record and need not question whether writing is inferior to speaking. Nonetheless, both of these issues need more attention in modern renditions of the history of rhetoric and its relation to dominant Western philosophies than they have been given. Our increasingly readerly definitions of rhetoric should be recognized as results from contributions that were made in changing images of writing and writers.

3 *Philosophy Confronts Writing*

Plato's Gorgias *and* Phaedrus

While it is commonplace in both rhetorical and literacy studies to point to Plato's critiques of rhetoric and of writing before countering them with support for either formal study, it is equally common for those in composition studies to overlook the precise ways in which the *Gorgias* and *Phaedrus* comment directly on their distinct subject. Both dialogues treat the cultural problem of endowing a relatively democratic mass of "students" with public and influential, but decidedly *written,* presence.

Up to this point, I have been looking at conditions for this presence without direct reference to surrounding discourses of philosophy and formal rhetoric that regularly include these dialogues. But for this study, as for any study attempting to theorize composition as a distinct field, an important fact is that from the first inscription of spoken language, writing has been embedded in philosophy and in rhetoric, always as the ugly stepsister, the "problem" of the visible text. While I am not proposing to read the Platonic dialogues or their comments on writing uniquely, other such readings have been taken seriously largely by literary scholars. Composition specialists also need a historical perspective on writing from philosophy to see that our assumptions about the primacy of writing are hard-won and even ambivalently held among ourselves. We may assume that textual studies are primary because our most immediate surroundings privilege written literature. But when we look at the places that composition, creative writing, and literary theory now hold, the three branches of textual studies that represent writing by the masses, their aesthetics, and writing about writing, it becomes clear that the mythology of the author identity of the writer, which is based in this philosophical tradition, still controls our willingness to endow seriousness and status to a text. This criteria for ranking has origins in orality and in oral rhetoric, for which Plato's dialogues provide the philosophical master texts.

Composition research and teaching have much at stake in acknowledging how ambivalence toward rhetoric and writing in traditional Western philosophy has created positions on the truth of a message and the validity of its source in written language that differ from those that define a contemporary writing subject. Our need for a discrete textual rhetoric and for its accommodations of ambivalence toward all the implications of writing is clarified by rereading these dialogues with this aim in mind. Consequently, Plato's dialogues are pivotal in the progress of this study. They comment on the changing aspects of literacy that the last chapter described while they reveal that issues around writing would inevitably and repeatedly come up in revisions of the practical art of the rhetorical theory that has always, if only implicitly, been held in tension with traditional philosophy. In their relation to changing possibilities for literacy, the dialogues' comments on fixity versus fluidity—on stating while refusing to claim a univocal meaning—access the many versions of literacy that ancient-through-Renaissance situations for the "writer" were to accumulate. And the comments of the *Gorgias* and *Phaedrus* on stable meaning and on writing also continue to appear, if in disguised forms, in changed rhetorical self-definitions that follow the progress of these literacies and of new technologies of writing. Consequently, I am rereading these sources to set the record a bit straighter about the confrontation between philosophical 'realism' and writing, just as I will reread a rhetorical history usually presented as a progress of "great men," not as a discontinuous chronology of formal rhetorical responses to actual writing.

Rhetoric has always been, at least in its most comprehensive definitions, an art of "presence," in all the senses that word entails. It addresses, in both natural and formal states, methods for bringing the otherwise silent person into a discourse "situation," a pointed moment of utterance that is consequentially set apart from the murmur of voices that temporally and substantially surround it.

When rhetoric was suddenly established as a codified system after the deposition of the tyrant Thrasybulus in Syracuse in 467 B.C. and the almost concurrent reformation of legal pleading in Athens in 462 B.C., it was part of a movement that by ancient standards instituted, if briefly, participatory democracy. George Kennedy, in *Classical Rhetoric and Its Christian and Secular Tradition from Ancient to Modern Times*, has noted that rhetoric by the end of the fifth century was a widely available "handbook literature" to which any citizen might turn to secure basic principles of public speaking.[1] It became, he says, socially important to be skilled in handbook teachings. Litigation, now argued by law between actual accusers and defendants, became a site for sophisticated entertainment. Service on large juries was sought by poorer citizens because of the fee involved, and watching the courts became analogous to attending other popular public events. Such an art could, at least in principle, guide any citizen who had not previously had the special status of poet, or singer. And as soon as this possibility existed, discrete dangers from the formerly silent audiences of traditional discourse were at hand.

While anyone would agree that the introduction of this public rhetoric created a problem and was immediately controversial, the nature of that problem has various explanations. As we have seen, internecine battles went on among Isocrates, Plato, and Aristotle, all of whom had vested interests in promoting their special brands of rhetorical teaching. We also know the poor reputation of the Sophists and of merely stylistic or mechanical teachers, said to be exploiters of the new need for "how-to" instruction. But competition among rhetorical codes and their teachers does not entirely explain the issues rhetoric raised in the context of new alphabetic literacy, which gave body to the Sophistic position that language, not essences, contains whatever contradictory reality we know. From the outset, an implicit political question was translated into a combat of philosophical theories. Perhaps, because it began at about the same time as the fairly rapid spread of Athenian literacy, codified rhetoric could put any individual in position to affect community customs and forms in discourse, not only in public situations but also separately and alone. And this positioning, which moved so quickly into an ambivalence toward writing in ancient primary literacy, implied that philosophical views of presence and authority—finally of reality and its authentic "communication"—had to be worked out.

To tie the difficulties around rhetoric to these political/ philosophical roots might appear farfetched if we do not remember how common it has been, especially for new "establishments," to legislate systems of education and to control public discourse institutions, as the restored English crown controlled the theatre or new totalitarian regimes control newspapers. These establishments usually discriminate between "important" and "ephemeral" contributions to public discourse, if they are not more obvious about their fears from "unlicensed" appeals to the public.

Even without this reminder, however, it is clear that a handbook rhetoric, written and circulated as a method that could theoretically stand in for listening to and directly imitating virtuosos, was immediately perceived in new democracies as a problem. On the one hand, if we agree with Havelock, the creation of philosophical discourse relied on a "written," not heroic, convention. But on the other, the possibilities inherent in writing invite dissent and unauthorized disseminations of elitist traditions. When rhetoric entered the gradual evolution from exclusively oral to mixed oral-literate culture, it at least implicitly raised questions about the status of the individual *composing* (whether in oral rehearsal of a speech, or in writing to prepare to speak publicly, or in writing to be read). New answers to these questions about status have changed the ways "rhetoric" is defined throughout its history, often because these are questions about "writing," the topic Plato chose in his critiques of rhetoric to oppose the methods and results of rhetoric to his realist philosophy.

I place "writing" in quotation marks because it is in the two dialogues explained here both an implicit and an explicit metaphor for the potential misdirections that can be taken from an impenetrable surface. That is, Plato took writing to be comparable in important ways to artificial, noninteractive "speechmaking," and treated both in terms of the new handbook art of rhetoric. Both dialogues address the implications, which Plato called "rhetorical," of allowing conventionalized modes of presentation to substitute for what he took to be actual reality, not a convention but an essence arrived at only by immediate teaching. This issue raised the specter of writing and its conventions and potential impersonality. It was still a relatively new technology, not yet entirely domesticated in the decidedly newer phenomenon of social literacy.

Both dialogues are also regularly cited as examples of early attacks on rhetoric and are generally lumped together with other ancient and later critiques of oratory and sophism like Aristophanes' *Clouds*. All of these criticisms attacked the glib, elaborate style of oratory that was taught and practiced in the new wave of popular speechmaking instruction like that given by Gorgias. But these dialogues took the philosophical, theoretical path. Both directly referred to public, popular, and, by implication, trivial instruction given by teachers like Gorgias and Lysias, the popular orator who is ridiculed in the *Phaedrus*, much as Pope later took on the dunces. But both more importantly emphasized the difficulty that codified rhetoric creates for the doctrine of heavenly forms that are eternal and real. In both, Plato exposed the relative falsity of immediate, situational topics and thus objected to the fundamental ground of rhetoric and of later textuality—contextualization and adaptation.

He thus attended, at every level, to writing. It symbolically re-creates the central problem of false and real in traditional Western philosophy, usually stated as the relation of the body to the soul.[2]

1   The *Gorgias*

Gorgias's own model speeches depended for their effects on schemes and tropes—parallelism, rhyme, antithesis, and syllabically equalized clauses. He is thought to have believed that speaking could have the same magical power as incantation, a matter on which Plato, as Eric Havelock argues in *Preface to Plato*, would have agreed, but without Gorgias's enthusiasm for the effect.[3] Gorgias was also a student of Empedocles, and wrote *On the Nonexistent, or On Nature*, a work whose title reveals his basic philosophical disagreement with Plato. It argues that nothing exists, that even if anything did exist man could not know it, and even if it could be known, it could not be communicated. Clearly, rhetorical relativism to the situation at hand would be congenial to Gorgias. He would not have been concerned about (nonexistent) 'reality' and its certain communication.

The *Gorgias* is confusing enough conceptually to suggest that the issues it raised were themes to be developed later. It systematically parodies rhetoric, its methods of evidence, and its proponents in the persons of Socrates' interlocutors, Gorgias, Polus, and Callicles. But the dialogue is surely not a set piece, a clearly drawn account of false rhetoric, the new evil in Athenian society. In a much more complicated fashion, it at once parodies and values the new systematic art of discourse, treating it more gingerly than common interpretations of this dialogue notice. Throughout, it opposes the method of fluid interaction to the method of making fixed statements, which "writing" set speeches entails.

As an argument, the dialogue's methods waffle between appearing to lead us gradually to a truth already in (Socrates') mind and appearing to be in the process of discovering new perspectives. It supplies technical rhetorical support for predetermined conclusions, but it also uses interactive methods from dialectic. The supposed content or message of the dialogue is equally undecided. One editor claims that the polemical point of the *Gorgias* is demonstrating that it is better to suffer wrong than to inflict it,[4] but accepting this interpretation would depend on oversimplifying Socratic dialogues into mere rhetorical statements, ignoring the conceptual dramas they are.

As a three-part (or act) encounter in which Gorgias, Polus, and Callicles are prominent by turns, the dialogue discusses oratory, the superiority of suffering to wrongdoing, and the relative evils of public life and true philosophy. Socrates ends by describing the eternal damnation to befall the person choosing to "pander" to public pleasure rather than to create instructive good. His neat concluding summary contradicts the movement and tone of the unsettled dialogue preceding it.

But we miss a great deal if we read this dialogue only sequentially, as a loose community of themes. Its statements are that oratory pleases, like cookery, rather than improves and instructs, like medicine; that punishment literally brings us "to justice" and thus is better than going free with impunity after wrongdoing; that philosophy pursued singly is preferable to political involvement in the community; that knowledge is better than, and different from, opinion. As we read, we often notice the dialogue's uses of oratory to demean oratory in convincing arguments that oratory is evil. We are taken by the dialogue's light and apparently diffuse treatments of a series of "great" ideas. But its quarrelsomeness and its uneven progressions toward, and away from, convincing cases about each of its themes leave us unsatisfied with the ideas it seems to collect. While there can be little doubt about the dialogue's antirhetorical tendency, it nonetheless persistently opposes its own cases for and against rhetoric.

This persistence of self-consciousness about making statements is worth noting. The dialogue's often-quoted definitions of oratory emerge from self-conscious comparisons and classifications. Calling rhetorical knowledge "a knack of convincing the ignorant that he knows more than the experts" (459), Socrates distinguishes "art" from "pandering." Pandering has many subdivisions; cookery, oratory, beauty-culture, and popular lecturing are "species of the same genus" (463). It would be quite improper Socrates says, using the dialectical method of *status* that became a rhetorical commonplace, to "say whether I think oratory honorable or the reverse before I have explained what it really is." Socrates attempts to clarify "what it really is" by relating it to the pairs of study related to the body and soul. Government deals with the soul; the body's art has not a name but two branches. "The members of each of these pairs," he says, are "training and medicine [the body's] legislation and justice" (464). The pseudo arts of pandering, cookery and its brothers, are dishonorable. Socrates reiterates the relation of cookery to medicine and of beauty-culture to physical training, lecturing about their boundaries:

> In short, I will put the matter in the form of a geometrical proportion—perhaps now you will be able to follow me—and say that cookery is to medicine as beauty-culture is to physical training, or rather that popular lecturing is to legislation as beauty-culture to training, and oratory to justice as cookery to

medicine. There is, I repeat, an essential difference between lecturing and oratory, but because they border on one another their practitioners are liable to be confused in the popular mind as occupying common ground and being engaged in the same pursuit; in fact lecturers and orators no more know what to make of one another than the world at large knows what to make of them. (465)

But the *Gorgias* persistently dislocates such ideas rather than summarizing them. The dialogue's disparate topics have more in common than this summary would reveal; its soul and body are not at odds. It has begun with an elaborate qualification and conditioning of the discourse to follow, a dramatic staging that is extremely self-conscious about its form, as is Socrates' long definition. Gorgias, who had already finished making a speech, is come upon by Socrates and Chaerephon, who question Callicles and Polus about whether Gorgias will be willing to answer questions. Socrates is concerned that the topics he wants to discuss with Gorgias may not interest the large group gathered for the speech now finished, but the spectators appear eager to hear, so we know that a large audience witnesses what follows.

More particularly, Socrates' first questions to Polus evoke and immediately cause a critique of long, sententious answers: "From what he has said it is clear to me that Polus has devoted himself much more to what is called oratory than to the art of conversation" (448). Socrates insists, here and throughout, on having a conversation, and as well on seemingly irrelevant and elaborate statements about methods of talking, interrupting, interpreting, and interacting. Gorgias is challenged to answer succinctly (449), and Socrates so often comments on the length and nature of his own or others' responses that it is worthwhile to point to a few of these comments as reminders of matter that has gone unnoticed in other explanations of the dialogue:

> SOCRATES: Would you be willing then, Gorgias, to continue the discussion on the present lines, by way of question and answer, and to put off to another occasion the kind of long continuous discourse that Polus was embarking on? . . . Show yourself willing to give brief answers to what you are asked. (449)

SOCRATES: That is just what I suspected you meant, Gorgias.
. . . My motive . . . is simply to help the discussion to progress towards its end in a logical sequence and to prevent
us from getting into the habit of anticipating one another's
statements because we have a vague suspicion what they are
likely to be, instead of allowing you to develop your argument in your own way from the agreed premises. (454)

SOCRATES: And if you think that we are mistaken in any of
our conclusions, I'm perfectly willing to take back anything
you like, but on one condition.

POLUS: What is that?

SOCRATES: That you keep in check the tendency to make long
speeches which you showed at the beginning of our conversation. (461)

SOCRATES: Is this a question or the beginning of a speech?
(466)

SOCRATES: Don't use hard words, my peerless Polus, if I may
address you for once in your own alliterative style. Prove my
mistake by your questions, if you still have any to ask, or
else let us change parts, and you do the answering. (467)

Similarly, although the dialogue appears to move in its
second and third parts to take up the relative virtues of avoiding wrongdoing versus suffering wrong, there are constant
references in these sections to various qualities of the
speeches: Callicles attacks Socrates for "all the extravagance
of a regular catch-penny speaker," calling his words an "out-
burst of claptrap" (482). He says, "there is no end to the
rubbish this fellow talks. Tell me, Socrates, aren't you
ashamed at your age of laying these verbal traps and counting
it a god-send if a man makes a slip of the tongue?" (489).
Gorgias asks Callicles to allow Socrates "to conduct the argument in his own way" (487), but Callicles only grudgingly
assents: "Go on with your fiddling little questions, since Gorgias will have it so" (497).

When Socrates defends himself, he calls Callicles a
"cheat" who constantly changes his ground. He had thought,
he says, that Callicles was a friend who would not mislead
him (499). The two carry on like the Bickersons:

CALLICLES: I don't feel the smallest interest in anything you
say. My only motive in answering you was to oblige Gorgias.

SOCRATES: What are we to do then? Leave the argument in
the air?
CALLICLES: You must decide that for yourself.
SOCRATES: One ought not to leave even a story half-told, they
say. It should be brought to a point and not left to go about
pointless. So answer the rest of my questions, and let our
discussion have a fitting end. (505)

Socrates further claims that he and Callicles have been talking
in "an endless circle of mutual misunderstanding" (517), and
that he has been compelled to "hold forth like a regular stump
orator." He has been led, he says, to make "my harangue
interminably prolix" (519). The only way out, Socrates thinks,
is to tell a story as proof:

CALLICLES: Well, since you have finished with all your other
points, you may as well round things off.
SOCRATES: Give ear then, as they say, to a very fine story,
which will, I suppose, seem fiction to you but is fact to me;
what I am going to tell you I tell you as the truth. (522–23)

These elaborate controls on, and references to, the discourse and its progress make two points. Socrates is insisting
from the outset on the conversational nature of the dialogue.
He missed Gorgias's speech, he inquires about the audience's
genuine interest rather than assuming that they want to hear
from an interlocutor in a formal question period, and he persistently pricks the discussant's "positions" with seemingly
wrongheaded redirection toward other points. He refuses the
set piece, both by requiring Gorgias's brevity and by reflexive
comments on his own long speeches. He has called himself,
after a long speech, a "regular stump orator." We are given
to understand that the dialogue's critique of oratory takes
exception to formal, noninteractive statements. Socrates' dialectical method of teaching depends on discourse strategies
that will lead to Truth. Discourse is interaction, not display.

But Plato also appears doubtful about this conclusion
and then makes another point. The interlocutors' have been
snippy, quarrelsome, and distracting in these supposedly
preferable brief interactions. They are more at odds at the end
of a discussion than they were at its polite beginning, so the
result of interaction is not necessarily to evenly illuminate a

truth, or Truth. Similarly, Plato has made it clear in the long definitional speech, which is usually taken to dismiss rhetoric as a superficial knack, that popular lecturing and a true oratory differ. At the close of the dialogue, Socrates both defines and must demonstrate the genuine art of the speech-toward-knowledge:

> Granted that there are two kinds of political oratory, one of them is pandering and base claptrap; only the other is good, which aims at the edification of the souls of the citizens and is always striving to say what is best, whether it be welcome or unwelcome to the ears of the audience. But I don't believe that you have ever experienced the second type; if you can point to any orator who conforms to it, lose no time in letting me into the secret of his identity.
>
> CALLICLES: Very well.
>
> SOCRATES: Then the good orator, being also a man of expert knowledge, will have these ends in view in any speech or action by which he seeks to influence the souls of men, in any gift which he may confer, and in any privation which he may inflict; his attention will be wholly concentrated on bringing righteousness and moderation and every other virtue to birth in the souls of his fellow-citizens, and on removing their opposites, unrighteousness and excess and vice. Do you agree? (503–4)

After this definition of good oratory, Socrates insists that Callicles "listen . . . while I recapitulate the argument from the start" (506), and proceeds on his own to rehearse the points he has achieved. He ends a few exchanges later with the closing myth of the afterlife, "a very fine story, which will, I suppose, seem fiction to you, but is fact to me" (523).

We have, then, both two arguments and two demonstrations of argumentation. Oratory may be used (as the *Phaedrus* even more clearly states) either superficially or knowledgeably, either to please or to instruct. Socrates insists, in intrusive metadiscourse throughout the dialogue, that genuine discourse demands interaction. However, this demand is held in tension with even more successful "speeches." Shared coming-to-know and polished, elaborated, single visions are juxtaposed, to the advantage of the long speeches. Socrates has, in effect, already forecast the nature of the rhetorical problem that the dialogue demonstrates. The importance of his opening speech thus becomes clearer: the dialogue to follow unites his and Gorgias's experiences as two elder teachers, who have witnessed many discussions like the one that is about to begin.

At great length, Socrates first says and then demonstrates that he and Gorgias must agree, on the basis of shared experience, that productive discourse consists of misunderstanding, the difficulty of defining terms, temptations to achieve verbal victories rather than understanding and—perhaps chiefly—the need for goodwill among the participants. What follows has demonstrated each of these difficulties and has resolved them only provisionally, sometimes by interpersonal appeals, sometimes by long arguments that are bracketed in the name of order and arrangement, sometimes by story and myth. Socrates ends firmly within the oral antecedents of his insistence on dialogue, speaking Homer's name. But he has also demonstrated his grasp of philosophical rhetoric and of its greater success in governing, even in his higher sense of governance.

This original critique of rhetoric differs markedly from those that are common today. It is perhaps useful to point out what the *Gorgias* does not say. It does not, for instance, criticize oratory for occasioning duplicity. It attributes great persuasive power to orators and points out that they may wish to please rather than edify or instruct the state. They are charged with lack of substance, or knowledge, and therefore with encouraging shallowness, but they are not accused of creating wrong beliefs in personally intended lies. Whatever ills rhetoric may bring, lying is not at issue. And this point is especially important in light of both Plato's political disaffection from Athenian government at the time and his competitiveness with other rhetorical schools. Had intentional duplicity been meant, the case would probably have been made.

More subtly, the dialogue's critique of oratorical knacks must be distinguished from its frequently supposed critique of mere stylistic embellishment. The *Gorgias* has relatively little to say about Sophistic style. Socrates twits Polus about his alliterations, calling him "peerless Polus," but he does not make much of the verbal forms practiced in popular oratory.

Turns of phrase are not the point. Phrases and words themselves are. They are, once spoken, taken by Socrates and the others to be a text. They are then "read" as suits the interlocutor. It is this more common quarrelsome ploy, whether taken up by a conversant or by a reader, that is demonstrated and called into question. And the ground for the question is that words that are separated from their speaker and his intent are "texts," the "speeches" that get right understanding into trouble.

It is therefore not rhetorical schemes and scheming but rather fixity versus fluidity that concerns Socrates in the *Gorgias*. The constant source of discord among these discussants is "knowing" what a person meant by interpreting only one single meaning of a word or phrase. Oratory itself, which was offstage at the dialogue's beginning, is also Gorgias's questioned as well as questionable occupation. It remains misdefined, ill defined, partially defined, and metaphorically defined, until it is in fact enacted by Socrates' long summary at the end of the dialogue. When even this final speech—which emphasizes the harmony, order, and arrangement of genuine oratory—is misunderstood, the case *against* a fixed "textual" language is confirmed. Socrates then resorts to myth and to the name of Homer, the fiction he admits is even more true than his explanation.

To say that "writing" is an implicit problem in the *Gorgias* is, then, to highlight the worry that both the set speeches that are so much the issue here and analogous written words are capable of later misinterpretation. This problem has everything to do with Socrates' reluctance to engage in anything but interpersonal learning, which oratory and writing persistently displace, as Isocrates' worries about his presence to his specifically written words indicated.

2   The *Phaedrus*

Ironically, myths and popular sayings again illuminate the problem of writing in the *Phaedrus*, which more directly shows the duality of the Socratic position toward writing or toward any fixed language. With few but significant exceptions, the *Phaedrus* has evoked receptions whose terms of

interpretation have come in for less opposition than they warrant. The problem of deciding which of the dialogue's topics
is its "real" message is imposed on the dialogue by most
readers, who respond with advocacy rather than critical explanations. The dialogue is said to be *about* rhetoric, love, and
knowledge; it is *against* rhetoric, which addresses immediate
matters of life and death placed before a community; it is *for*
knowledge and the soul. The either/or dichotomies that most
readers have derived from the dialogue arise not only from
our natural desires to classify or to resolve any text but from
the dialogue's internally unsettled points. But the *Phaedrus*
does not and could not, in view of its historical relation to the
spread of writing, encourage resolutions about its subjects.

These subjects are persistently varied. Socrates and
Phaedrus meet outside the city, in a pointedly rural and personal rather than organized or arranged setting. They walk
from spot to spot, imitating the mental progress prescribed by
rhetorical treatments of memory, which recommend that the
speaker "hang" pieces of a speech in a well-remembered locale
for retrieval as he spoke.

Phaedrus appears to be reciting a speech about love
that Lysias, one of Gorgias's counterparts, has recently given.[5]
In the dialogue that follows, Socrates listens to this speech,
which argues that it is better to be "persuaded" by a nonlover
than a lover, then matches it with one of his own, then recants
in the name of conscience and delivers yet a third speech on
the divine madness of love. Having brought himself, and
Phaedrus, around to true discourse, he discusses its qualities:
its fit of parts to the whole and of form to substance. But he
ends with a myth about the invention of writing that shows
that writing destroys memory, which throughout the dialogue
has been cast as the valued link between the world of substance and the "knowledge of forms." Recollection, finally
seen to be destroyed by writing, is the source of individuals'
union with the true and the beautiful above.

Both Stanley Fish in *Self-Consuming Artifacts* and Jacques
Derrida in *Disseminations* have read the *Phaedrus* as a dialogue
that takes us, persistently and repeatedly, away from the decidable, the definite, and a stated single meaning. Both point
out that the dialogue works with a problem that engenders but

cannot supply solutions. Their views supply the best rubric for understanding this early philosophical comment on the trouble with rhetoric as a problem of "writing."[6] That is, the dialogue does engage and then change a reader's understanding of a series of issues that early Greek rhetoric and rhetoric to the present persistently raise. Each time an answer is articulated, or "written," its context for application, or its adequacy in this context, is challenged. In the *Phaedrus*, writing itself is questioned as a specific concern. But the issue is not technological. More explicitly than in the *Gorgias*, the *Phaedrus* implicitly and explicitly compares rhetoric to systematized writing. It philosophically raises this comparison to explore metonymically the central problem in traditional Western thought, artificiality versus reality, form versus substance, body versus spirit.

The *Phaedrus* dramatizes actions, not just ideas. It attends with equal care to its setting (outside the city, where Socrates rarely goes) and to its movement from one to another bracketed topic. The speakers provide clear demarcations between topics and call attention to the self-contained, established nature of each of them. The two men repeatedly interrupt to note the surrounding in which the discussion is occurring: Did Boreas carry Oreithylia off just here?; Can we find a shady spot?; Shall Socrates leave or come back to give his third speech?; Shall they chat in the noon sun like two resting slaves or keep talking to the tune of watching crickets? The dialogue is thus conspicuously homey while aggressive about the relation of the interlocutors to a particular rather than generalizable time and place.

The issue at the outset is whether Phaedrus has memorized the progression of Lysias's speech, of which he carries a copy under his cloak. In this exchange, the relation of lover to beloved is also introduced; the long roll of papyrus under the youth's cloak and Socrates' demand to see what is there begin the dialogue's sustained playful, ironic tone, which will be mentioned explicitly at its end. Phaedrus says that he cannot reproduce Lysias's speech "in a manner worthy of the master," and Socrates chides in response that he knows that Phaedrus has listened more than once, begged Lysias for repetition, and then reread parts until the whole was mastered. Phaedrus is here, Socrates knows, to practice, but he has met "a man who had an abnormal appetite for hearing good talk"[7] and has become coy about reciting for him. But Phaedrus insists that his problem is memory: "the trouble is that I haven't got the words by heart." He can summarize main points, but he has not learned the speech word by word. Thus all the elements of discourse in a bifurcated, oral-literate culture are brought up right away: mentoring, written words, listening, memory, and the difference between "knowing" a truth and "knowing" specific words for it.

While Socrates and Phaedrus look for a place to sit and read the speech together, they speculate about myths said to have occurred on this spot: Whether Boreas carried Oreithylia off or whether, as Socrates "rationalizes," she was at play with Pharaceia and pushed by the North Wind over a cliff is not, Socrates says, important to him. He has not yet come, he says, to understand himself. "I leave such subjects alone and adopt the common view about them" (229). Thus, the two, who have come away from the oratorical audience and the city's scholars, thematically establish the disparity between "common views" and genuine knowledge, which Socrates localizes in self-knowledge.

Before a word of Lysias's speech or comments about it begin, the dialogue has raised issues at the heart of rhetorical problems. The "common view" that is derided in the *Gorgias*, the physical and intellectual separation of an individual from society that the *Gorgias* addressed, and the primacy of knowledge are all readdressed, as the context in which rhetoric, and love, must be discussed. As in the beginning of the *Gorgias*, when Socrates insisted on "just talk" rather than an official question period after Gorgias's speech, understanding is identified with intimacy.

Phaedrus reads Lysias's speech, which Socrates analyzes afterward as having "clear and precise" language (234) but as being a poor example of discourse on this subject. His analysis of the piece is technical, to the point, and accurate:

> To me, in fact, Phaedrus—if you don't disagree—it seemed that the author was saying the same thing two or three times, as though he weren't capable of saying a great deal on a single topic—or perhaps he wasn't especially interested in the matter.

I thought it quite a virtuoso performance, to show himself capable of saying the same thing in two different ways, and both of them excellently.

. . . . For example, to take the present topic: who do you suppose, in stating that one ought to comply with a non-lover rather than a lover, could omit to praise the prudence of the one and to blame the folly of the other? These are, of course, commonplaces; what else could one say? We must . . . forgive their use, applauding the arrangement, not the inventiveness of their author; and when it is a matter of topics that are not commonplaces, that are difficult to invent, in addition to his arrangement his inventiveness also should be applauded. (235–36)

For a man who was ridiculed for not knowing how to "put the question" when on the Council (*Gorgias* 474), Socrates is well versed in rhetorical analysis. He understands the techniques and descriptive nomenclature taught by the same rhetoricians he attacks in both of these dialogues, and can confront this set piece by Lysias on its own ground. Lysias's "knack" is wanting here.

Socrates next offers his own version of this argument. His "First Speech" begins with a narration (Once Upon a Time . . .) unlike Lysias's incomprehensibly abrupt "What my circumstances are, you know; and you have heard how I believe they should be settled to our best advantage." Socrates interrupts himself to note that he is giving "the impression of being truly divine" by speaking dithyrambically and ends "because I had begun to utter epic verse." He need not finish by recounting the positive side of the negative qualities of the lover. Phaedrus, or any audience, could imagine how the speech would go on. "For each evil that we have reproached in the one, there is corresponding good in the other" (241). He is impressed beyond words by his own artfulness.

But he is also disgusted back into words by this speech. It was false; love is a god. The lover improves the soul of the beloved; their discourse moves each toward divine insight.

Socrates recounts this progression first philosophically, or abstractly, describing the soul, its self-motion, and its progress toward unmediated reality. But his second speech relies heavily on the "story of heaven," the narrative of the animated soul (246).

In his description of the reality that the soul seeks, he stresses the directness of such knowledge: "Reality lives, without shape or color, intangible, visible only to reason, the soul's pilot" (247). In the complex story of how humans attain heaven and the direct immediacy of vision that follows this attainment, Socrates says that only memory connects the reincarnated soul and its heaven-bound progression. Only memory endows the philosopher's mind with wings, so that it can gaze at light in purity, "not disfigured by this so-called body . . . imprisoned in it like oysters in a shell." Socrates venerates memory: "Let this tribute, then, be paid to memory, which has caused us to enlarge upon it now, yearning for what we once possessed" (250).

Phaedrus, like the reader reconditioned by it, now praises this speech as most beautiful of the three. Lysias, he confides, is falling on hard times, is branded a "speechwriter." "It's possible," he says, "that from pride he may stop writing."

> SOCRATES: Young man, that is an absurd notion. You are completely mistaken in your friend if you think he's afraid of noisy abuse. Perhaps, too, you believe that the abuser intended what he said as a reproach?
>
> PHAEDRUS: It seemed so, Socrates. You know yourself that the most influential and dignified people in political life are ashamed to write speeches or leave behind them any prose writing through fear of being called "sophists" by posterity. (257)

The point, Socrates says, is not that speech writing is bad, but that writing bad speeches is bad: "the disgrace comes in when the speaking and the writing is not good, when it is, in fact, disgracefully bad" (258).

Now it appears to be a sudden change in content to move from the devotional speech Socrates has just given to discussing how we distinguish good writing from bad writing. And Plato further seems to interrupt with the story of the transformation of men who admired the Muses into crickets, who now in the heat of midday sing around the two conversants.

But these epideictic crickets report to the Muses about which mortals most deserve honor, and this worthiness has to do with language. Socrates especially notes Calliope and

Urania, whom the crickets tell about as those who "honor the art of these Muses who, above all the others, sing the most sweetly in their preoccupation with heavenly things and with discourse mortal and divine" (259). The issues of mediating between earth and heaven, of continuing to converse rather than take a midday snooze, and of the heavenly patronage given history and poetry are focused in this seemingly playful legend, which does not interrupt but refocuses the progress of the conversation. Phaedrus responds with "Well, then, let's talk!" (259).

What follows in large measure alludes, in rewritten fashion, to the topics of the *Gorgias*. Phaedrus says he has heard that it is not necessary "to learn what is really just and true, but only what seems so to the crowd who will pass judgment . . . for it is from what seems to be true that persuasion comes, not from the real truth" (260).

Here again, the problem rhetoric raises is not that the rhetor necessarily falsifies what he knows to be true but that he will inevitably, by virtue of focusing on particular situations, misrepresent reality. He may, Socrates jokes, try to convince Phaedrus to buy a horse to go to war, but persuade him instead that the donkey is a horse because "neither of us know what a horse is." The rhetor may not *know* the Truth and thereby may persuade the city that an absolute evil is a contingent good. Socrates is not saying, and does not say so elsewhere, that the lie originates in the conscious will of the speaker, but that it originates in the speaker's ignorance of, and inattention to, philosophy and love, which lead to true knowledge. He explains that "we have insulted the art of making speeches more freely than we should have."

But Socrates also advances the claim that rhetoric is not an art, that it is only "an artless routine," the knack, or trick, defined in the *Gorgias*. The two agree to consider its status, and in the process, Socrates offers definitions: "rhetoric, taken as a whole, is an art of influencing the soul through words, not merely in the law courts and all other public meeting places, but in private gatherings also?" (261). Phaedrus says he has not heard that at all. Rhetoric, he had thought, is confined to law courts and public speaking.

But Socrates replies, in a definition directly parallel

to Aristotle's in the *Rhetoric*, that because contention is an issue in philosophy as well (he cites Zeno's paradoxes), it pertains in all kinds of speaking. "It will be an art by which one will be able to produce every possible sort of resemblance between comparable objects as well as one by which one can expose the attempts of others to produce resemblances through obfuscation" (261). Here we see the rhetorical "versionality" that Gerald Bruns explained, pointed out in the context of versions of Lysias's speech. Fortunately, the two have at hand the examples of both this speech and Socrates'; they can investigate how a man who knows the truth, but plays with words to lead the audience astray, can use rhetoric.

What follows is a clear, systematic lesson in rhetoric. It includes the necessity of first defining terms, and the requirement that discourse be organic, "like a living creature." It must have body, head, and feet, "all composed in such a way that they suit both each other and the whole" (264).

But it is also possible to compose so that the order of the parts makes no difference. The inscription on Midas's tomb demonstrates and, as Phaedrus says, makes fun of evaluations based on organism:

A maiden of bronze am I, placed on the tomb of Midas
So long as water flows, so long as trees grow tall
Here I abide on this tomb of tears
I declare to the passer-by that HERE LIES MIDAS. (264)

Any of these lines may equally well begin the inscription, and while he wants to pass on to the next part of the analysis, Socrates alludes to the visualization of writing by noting that "it seems to me that there was something in them that those who want to study rhetoric might find worth examining" (264).

The juxtaposition of these cautionary lines with the elegantly stated, opposing definition of rhetoric's art is followed by a similar division of the two speeches Socrates gave on love. One defined madness on the "left" and further subdivided the subject to show its sinister character; the other divided it and proceeded on the right. But this is the method, they remind themselves, of dialectic; rhetoric remains elusive.

They note that the rhetorical handbooks require a set pattern of arrangement, not the organic rigor of dialectics. They recount the various contributions of writers on the subject: covert allusion, indirect praise, indirect censure. This catalogue is presented as a hodgepodge of self-parody, capped by Prodicus's claim that he had learned "to make speeches neither long nor short, but of reasonable length." ("Very clever, Prodicus," says Phaedrus.) The two continue this catalogue: intentional dittology, gnomic and figurative clarification, and noun equivalents in the interest of poetic elegance. And there is the *Correct Diction* of Pythagoras.

This list is ridiculous, and more so for its historical accuracy. The devices of speechmaking and elegance are listed to their detriment. As their number accumulates, the rhetoric lesson moves further and further from the unity of purpose and form that was earlier described as merely appended or attached to the "method." But those who are ignorant of dialectic, the method of definition and division Socrates advocated just before, are basically struck with believing that technique is enough. They teach it and "think their job is done."

The true art of rhetoric is reached, Socrates says, by the supplement of "leisurely discussion, by stargazing . . . about the nature of things" (269). When this supplement (which is not writing and can in no sense be "written") is engaged, rhetoric turns out to be *like* medicine. "In both cases you must analyze a nature, in the one that of the body, in the other that of the soul, if you are going to proceed scientifically, not merely by empirical routine" (269). Rhetoric is not limited to cookery but, like medicine, may poison as well as improve, depending on whether advocates of each know the nature of the particular problem at hand and know it in the philosophical terms that Socrates insists on. And discussion—immediate interactions between individuals—is the only way this knowledge may be found. A "science of rhetoric" needs an accurate description of the soul.

Like Socrates, then, we must make finer distinctions than current discourse studies have made if we are to understand historical or intuitive problems with rhetoric and its true nature. We can easily enough accept "common opinion" about what this dialogue says about rhetoric's nature and its dangers: it is a mere technique of manipulating language and its equated listener/readers; it participates in public and political worlds and is therefore ignoble; it makes the worse appear the better case; it distorts the nature of things when it is not organically composed discourse.

But Socrates has not let us rest with these bad influences. Rhetoric as practiced by itinerant teachers, Gorgias and his brothers, is indeed technique only, the preoccupation with words that occasion misunderstanding. But there is another rhetoric, the counterpart of dialectic. Both arts may be used (as Socrates himself demonstrated by virtue of making his first, dialectic but untrue, speech) to lead the soul toward or away from congruence with divine Truth. As we saw in the *Gorgias*, contention and discussion permeate all interactions, whether public or private, political or philosophical, particular or general. Consequently, rhetoric may not simply be the public speaking technique isolated from philosophical discussion. Both speechmaking and dialectics may be learned as techniques, whether the pupil has natural talent or not.

Rhetoric's reputation, in short, is poor because it is seen to have to do only with the surface of things—the style, figures, schemes, tropes, and devices of mechanistic organization, the *words* without souls that embody—or *dis*embody— discourse. When words are separated from their substantive and interpersonal contexts, they become effective, or not, only on and in the surface they take to be their domain. Cases may be made one way or another and approved or rejected without reference to the essential relation of speech to mankind: The purpose of speech, Socrates has said, is to lead the soul. Although he has insisted on the dialectics of dividing the question, or subject, throughout the dialogue, Socrates persistently reaffirms the evil of dividing speech—form from content, content from essence, purpose from audience, and (especially in his horror of this first rejection of love) message from man.

We can imagine, then, an art of rhetoric as Socrates describes—a mixture of teaching and holding forth, questioning and speechmaking, interactions and provisional conclusions—that leads us for all our souls' sakes from a particular case to a new perception of reality.

But there are problems, again, with this.

There is writing.

Despite Derrida's renovating focus on it, the significance of writing in the *Phaedrus* is easily overlooked or dislocated, for many reasons. It is often asserted that Socrates never wrote, and that we know this because Plato did. Some readers of the *Phaedrus* in fact interpret the dialogue as a comment on this difference, thinking that it argues subtly in favor of writing, against Socrates' dislike of it. Ronna Burger, for instance, in *Plato's Phaedrus: A Defense of the Philosophical Art of Writing* argues that the "writing" Socrates describes, Egyptian hieroglyphs depicting animals and objects, is less capable of leading the soul to truth than new alphabetic writing in fifth-century socially literate society. Alphabetic writing, she claims, is more democratic and alive, a better mediator between speech and soul.[8]

But even if this interpretation were universally accepted, it would still require an act of imagination to understand how the issues around writing that are addressed so late in the dialogue fit in a still oral-literate (as opposed to "semiliterate") culture. Writing was still unstable, a technology but not yet an institutionalized topic. Its uses were new and startling, like Phaedrus's awkward transportation of the copy of Lysias's speech. Its easy accessibility in our terms was unimagined, as was a necessary connection between it and acts of composition by poets and orators. It properly worried both Socrates and Plato.

As ancient references demonstrate, words written down addressed "audiences" even when sent to correspondents; they usually did not record entirely private matters. The free-floating space within which we notice "a note," "another article," or "a rough draft," the space now defined theoretically as intertextuality, was only just coming to be in relation to actual written discourse. Written texts were not a world with their own history and capacity for extensive structural and formal, word-by-word analyses. A document was "an instance" or example not of writing but of *a writing*, conveying a particular person's intention in a public situation.

Consequently, the *Phaedrus*'s references to writing require careful rereading. The myths that begin, center, and close the conversation coherently comment on the topics that are more philosophically presented, pointing to the explicit problem with writing, its relation to memory. Socrates' opening comment about Oreithylia's fate involves Pharaceia, whose name suggests the common Greek "drug," "remedy," and "poison." The word will be applied again to writing's questionable preservation/destruction of memory. Oreithylia may have been, Socrates speculates, carried off by Boreas or distracted by Pharaceia. This "scientific" hypothesis, contrary to myth or story, foreshadows other references to writing. It leads away from the self and away from self-knowledge that Socrates emphatically wants *instead of* scientific hypotheses. Writing falsifies and distracts from the actual. It is a "drug" that led Socrates from the city (230d–e). Oreithylia forgot herself, or so a supposedly scientific hypothesis suggests.

Similarly, the crickets reporting to the Muses are not mere signs of the heat but are also men so drugged by songs and discourse that they had died and were "treated," or remedied. They report to Muses, whose mother is Memory. They are thrice removed from the link of body to soul that Socrates venerates. At the center, precisely halfway through, we find the discussion of logography—writing, the "ghost" of the spoken word (275c) that Phaedrus says orators avoid. And again later, placed as parts of the body whose senses Socrates has temporarily valued, at the supporting foot of the discourse, is writing.

The closing myth of writing's invention by Teuth shows writing to be not a simple remedy or prescription for memory. It destroys memory while preserving it; it captures while distorting meaning. Writing subjects itself to strangers—their "readings" and misinterpretations. It embodies while it disembodies words. It cures as it kills. By virtue of its immortality, it does not necessarily oppose the mortal or the body. What is body is not soul and paradoxically a written preservation of the soul is, finally, only body, an inscription.[9]

Writing, Socrates says, is the bastard without the protection of the father, the origin. Its brother, legitimate speech, emanates from the individual. But writing is only the ghost of legitimate discourse: "The man who has real knowledge of justice and beauty and goodness will not, when he's in earnest, resort to a written form and inscribe his seeds in water, and in inky water at that; he will not sow them with a pen, using words which are unable either to argue in their own defense when attacked or to fulfill the role of a teacher in presenting the truth" (276).

Socrates develops this metaphor of seeds, equating writing with the forcing bed of a horticulturist, who may well want a temporary "show" but would never plant crops for quick and ephemeral harvest. But the metaphor already contains enough allusiveness to remind us of *its* origins within the dialogue: the seeds of philosophy sown by the true lover lead to the divine as these seeds of writing will not. The pen is not the appropriate means of implanting seeds of truth, nor is that scroll Phaedrus hid under his cloak.

If we can assume a unity among themes in the head, center, and feet in the dialogue's body and the tensions that new writing necessarily created for self-conscious oral-literate Greek culture, writing becomes much of what this dialogue is "about." The identity/difference between body and soul *is* writing—it memorializes and memorizes. That is, it serves memory, the link to heaven and mother of all discourse. But for Socrates and later Greeks, memory is alive, a product of dialogues rather than of treatises. It is spatial and fluid, more likely to be the circle of the Zodiac or the scenes on Achilles' shield than to be hierarchical outlines. Memory is achieved by looking in locales, the places passed on a common walk, visible in a familiar room, or under Phaedrus's cloak. It is not achieved by memorizing textual features but by recurrence, rhythm, and repetition.

Socrates therefore objects to abstract, linear forms that can be imposed on anyone's memory and may generate ideas as readily as they organize them. The lines of written organization could, he saw, appropriate the thoughts and feelings of the writer and the writer's personal perception of a subject. Thus, what appears to aid memory opposes it: the same symbols are used in writing to represent a variety of meanings detached from their origin. Writing is all body, no soul. Writing also freezes; it drugs our active movement through love to reunion with heaven. It leaves the word, which is the soul expressed through speech, defenseless. Like crickets, it repeats without knowing. Writing as fixity is the essence of sophistry—a knack, a mere technique.

Socrates' statement is not alone among early debates about the ambivalent value of writing. As we have seen, Isocrates argued that writing his speeches was an excellent aid to composition and memory and not necessarily destructive to spontaneous delivery. But this particular statement of the problem of writing in the *Phaedrus* is most closely tied to the issue it represents in philosophy, the relation of body to soul, or inside to outside, or surface to internal, organic, meaning. We are as distant from free soul in our oyster-shell bodies as writing is from what we "mean," or vividly for Plato, what we may be taken to have meant.

The *Phaedrus* asserts that true speech is not fixed, either in handbook rhetoric or in writing. This was a problem for a culture in which writing was a novelty, as it is in our times, when we now confront implications from the capacity of inscriptions to re-collect what has been distributed, transmitted, and scattered among a world made of texts. Plato's dialogue fits well into later direct critiques of writing. Writing was at first a new, transitional, dangerous-to-stability technology; it is now so well established as to have relocated soul in genuinely written, always quoted "essences." These are parallel conditions for writing, intriguing Plato and Derrida equally because neither philosopher assumes the power of an "authorizing" voice that writing became in its first ascendancy, as a secondary literacy developed. The dialogue is ahead of a history of writing at whose feet we now sit, explaining the many-handed *logos* of equally medicinal and decadent textuality.

In neither of these dialogues do we find the sort of resolution that their current status as authoritative "texts" from our philosophical father would lead us to assume we could. And that is, as I have been arguing along with Fish and Derrida, their point. Uncomfortable as it makes us, both the *Gorgias* and *Phaedrus* pose the specific problematic of textuality: we may only temporarily overcome inevitable misreadings and inevitable misstating. The willingness to make statements despite their slippery instability depends on local fictions, the frames we place around discourse to impel its apparent, but in fact absent, stable meanings. In both dialogues, the fluidity of personal interactions outside the "city" of knowledge or formal oratory reveal that "taking positions," "making points," and even artfully composing language will be only partially successful attempts at full presence.

Further personal interactions may undo or solidify these successes, as the quarrels in the *Gorgias* and the friendship in *Phaedrus* demonstrate. But when these temporary successes (and, we infer from Socrates' assessment of Lysias's "bad writing," similar temporary failures) are *written*, their instability is magnified. Only the trust associated with myth or religious conviction overcomes the instability of written language, as Plato, the banisher of poets, and our modern myths of authorship tell us.

4 Writing Confronts Rhetoric
Changing Definitions

Theories of formal rhetoric are always concerned with the possibilities for discourse that philosophical, social, and technological circumstances define. They have not been independent of cultural facts, which now invite us to consider an inevitable textual rhetoric. But this perception has repeatedly been forestalled by commitments to the root metaphor of the speaking subject under realist philosophy and by what amounts to a paradoxical priority for this subject as a unitary source of "meaning" in rhetorical theory, the antirealist companion to this philosophy through time. We have many oblique accounts in rhetoric of the history of the speaking subject, who is always in these sources taken to be unfortunately attenuated, not enlarged, by written discourse situations. Writing, we have imagined, must be overcome, not celebrated, for its places in a series of new discourse possibilities. Consequently, traditional accounts usually ignore, or appear to appropriate, the problematics of language itself, which enter the picture the moment that language may be inscribed. They set aside inscribed language at every historical point where writing has touched relations between philosophy and rhetoric. We have been left with elaborate descriptions that characterize unitary rhetoric and its "good men speaking" as unfortunately embattled, fragmented victims.

I am, on the contrary, rereading rhetorical history to allow writing and the needs of the written subject their place as agents of change. While this account may appear to reiterate the teleological progress of great men contributing to a "tradition," it instead describes a disjunctive chronology in which gaps and slippages have everything to do with the changing literacies that were described earlier. In light of the problematics of written language Plato addressed, an alternative history of rhetoric gathers technological possibilities into a positive account of overt appropriations and covert resistances to written language in theories of spoken discourse. Actual writing, even in its stepsister role, has confronted oral theories of composition, inevitably modifying them in ways that call on composition specialists to assert their particular perspective on the written subject and to find a textual rhetoric capable of discriminating this subject's fictionalized presence to discourse.

It may be valuable for rhetorical studies to see how this approach might diminish its persistent nostalgia for unified ancient rhetoric. But whatever results appear in historical rhetorical studies, writing must be considered if the continuing relation of rhetoric to composition is to be sorted out. Relating rhetoric to composition as father text to spurious copy is inadequate, for rhetoric is a bit less, more, and differently relevant to changing practices in discourse education than we usually realize. It has always been concerned with the issue Plato addressed, a dislocation from immediacy into set speeches, and with the concurrent problem of impenetrable surfaces. From Augustine to the present, rhetoric as both a theoretical and an educational discourse has addressed a lost "past" represented by the speaking subject while deferring to new discourse situations created by writing. But in its persistent claims to transmit its doctrines directly in the voices of its major figures, it uses a highly formulaic process of self-definition that leaves it, as an enclosed discourse, less relevant to writing than its chief supporters in composition admit. Its own divisions, expansions, and eventual fragmentations are treated with the implicit anxiety about change that controls the *Gorgias* and *Phaedrus*. Thus, the social problems of writing have been absorbed in successive restatements and renewals of the field that now need to be read differently, to account for their relationship to writing.

1   Premodern Definitions of Rhetoric: Shifting Responses to Writing

All ancient definitions of rhetoric emphasize thinking and speech, whose complex interrelation we can accept while noticing that both of these processes reside in the orator him-self. Early rhetoric was taught to and blamed on a person speaking, not bestowed on an independent text or on a more or less receptive and knowing audience. Aristotle's complex analysis of the arguments suitable to particular audiences (*Rhetoric*, bk. 2), which is often called the first psychological treatise, was intended to instruct the speaker, not an audience or the analyst of discourse.

Rhetoric in its first categorical manifestations is a matter of personal development, of *someone* fitting thought and utter-ance to purpose and situation. The orator cannot step outside himself but rather takes the outside into himself. He persuades others to his views, which are not singular or idiosyncratic but are publicly owned as the result nonetheless of *his* powers and practice. In this view of discourse, a speaker may be a mouthpiece, but always for his own chosen perspectives within a community's conventional views. He shares an inter-nally constructed representation, his artistry.

But early on, this premise of the first oral rhetorics required change in light of the matter and practice of dis-course. Augustine's rhetoric that is not a rhetoric is an ideal example. Augustine, who had among other frivolities taught rhetoric in Rome before his conversion, was at pains to substi-tute Christian for pagan literature and methods. But he needed a version of rhetoric to interpret scripture and to guide preaching. *On Christian Doctrine*'s preface refutes opponents who might discount such an adaptive project. He proposed to write a new rhetoric—an interpretive guide to the world's relation to God, to "things and signs." He began, in "Book Fourth," by denying that he intended to write a rhetoric at all:

> 2. In the first place, then, I wish by this preamble to put a stop to the expectations of readers who may think that I am about to lay down rules of rhetoric such as I have learnt, and taught too, in the secular schools, and to warn them that they need not look for any such from me. Not that I think such rules of no use, but that whatever use they have is to be learnt elsewhere.[1]

Augustine then defined rhetoric, at least implicitly, in a dualis-tic way. It is both the armor of the defenders of the faith (2;

bk. 4) and a set of rules for eloquence that, he emphasizes, need not be studied by those who already have the native wit to catch on to them by reading and practice (3; bk. 4).

Augustine takes on a persona that is unusually common in treatments of rhetoric, that of the insider who is newly outside tradition. His is the first theoretical separation of rhetorical methods from a discourse's content, and especially of the speaker's character from his discourse's quality, although these separations are implicit in the Platonic dialogues on rhetoric. But in direct opposition to Quintilian, whose definition and doctrines had prescribed developing the rhetor's character, Augustine radically suggested that a preacher might credibly speak in another's words. Because the manifest energy and persuasiveness of the Christian message is in the Spirit speaking through the person, not in the ethos of the speaker, Augustine could assert new, instrumental views of thinking, speaking, or of writing.

He goes on after his disclaimers to review overtly rhetorical principles. For example, "Chapter XII—The aim of the orator, according to Cicero, is to teach, to delight, and to move. Of these, teaching is most essential." Among rhetorical precepts, he intersperses Christian principles of wisdom, as in "Chapter XV—The Christian teacher should pray before teaching." So the rhetoric he wrote was a revisionist rhetoric. It placed *inventio*, the systematic discovery of appropriate ideas, in the Spirit or in other sermons, not in the Christian rhetor's personal power.

Augustine's work signaled the major relocation of "rhetoric" that paved the way, substantially and methodologically, for those who followed him. "Rhetoric" is now capable of power through the authority of a text, not only through the ethos of its speakers. Thus, his rhetoric, as John Freccero has also said of the *Confessions*, provided the first glimmer of what has become the paradox of an individual "seen both as subject and object,"[2] as a self separated from self that can both "speak" and be "spoken by" higher authority. Slight attention to writing in earlier rhetoricians' work is, with Augustine, located at the heart of theory. This is the first of many bifurcations in statements of what a formalized subject of rhetoric and the writer *is*. Like its followers, this branching was only implicitly articulated, but it nonetheless differentiated rhetoric to aid a person's speaking from rhetoric to transmit "qualities" within discourse. These qualities for Augustine are Christian truths; they become, as further examples show, stylistic eloquence, displays of logic, or methods of "communication."

Augustine's displaced rhetoric is also the first expression of what we might call a postoral locus for presence. Unlike earlier rhetoric, which united human sources of discourse with the created "text" and its reception by an audience, his rhetoric announced that thought and speech might be programmatically separated, that they are not necessarily or causally linked. Early rhetoric had been designed to shape speech that was not, for the Greeks at least, distinct from thought—which was itself intended, where intended at all, to shape "what I want to say." In early communities that were still arguing about writing's uses and implications, the sources, facts, and audiences for "rhetoric" were united in this intentional aspect of its definitions. An orator's character, his words, and their result had to be comprehended in relation to each other, as Isocrates' difficulties with recording his "presence" show.

The stage had been set for this relocation of presence by the demise of social literacy in Rome and the prevalent Christian view that the word must be powerfully formed and can be powerfully effective despite its speaker's talent, skill, or morality. Following Augustine, medieval rhetoric continued to relocate discourse in such Christian concerns. In many of its preoccupations, medieval rhetorical training is characteristically re-presentational. The sermon and the letter, for instance, were added to early rhetorical categories as forms that can *stand in for* their authors, whose literal presence they were said to capture in the forms and formats developed to make writing trustworthy. The particular formats, terms of address, and salutations in these genres relied on the newly possible division of a speaker from a text and its audience. Rhetoric became *a way* to say something, not a unified faculty within a univocal, originating source. We have seen this effect already in medieval writing, a discrete textual literacy.

Post–Gutenberg Renaissance rhetorics separated these new "parts" of rhetoric even further, not in a "trend" but in response to a clearly disjunctive technology. They divided the domains of classical rhetoric into separable studies or reincorporated them in logic, dialectics, and philosophy. Such treatments of rhetoric implicitly celebrated duplicable texts, which separated "speakers" from their words even further than manuscript culture could. Even newer rhetorics approved of relegating invention and arrangement to the study of logic or emphasized figures, schemes, and tropes—the features of written texts that print had stabilized.

In Erasmus's *De Copia* (1550), for example, the word "rhetoric" is hard to find. In this extraordinarily popular and influential version of the subject, which went through 150 editions in the sixteenth century, "the rhetorician's art"[3] associated with probability is envisioned as "thoughts and words overflowing in a golden stream" (11). Here (and in most of Erasmus's immediate followers in both Latin and English), rhetoric is treated as the figures, schemes, and tropes applied to creating seemingly infinite variations on any statement. Finding and ordering arguments are treated as "Copia of Thought" (bk. 2). With suitable acknowledgment of Quintilian, Cicero, and other literary and oratorical sources, Erasmus nonetheless described an entirely new content for rhetoric, an infinitely fertile, close duplication of signs.

This sort of relocation has much to do, as do Peter Ramus's complex charts and diagrams of knowledge, with writing. As Terrance Cave has pointed out, placing rhetoric in the realm of *copia* "adumbrates a theory of writing as an activity at once productive and open-ended, escaping the limits which formal treatises of rhetoric and dialectic attempt to impose on it."[4] Erasmus's rhetoric was, that is, a replacement of rhetoric into the same concerns expressed in Renaissance critical theories, where oratorical presence was reconstrued for written authorship. Erasmus took *copia*, an oratorical ideal at base, into a textual world, where it might eventually become an oral residue.

Another similar instance of restating rhetoric under the influence of print was the tactic of Peter Ramus, who emphatically did not avoid definitions. His broad influence on rhetorical method has been variously perceived to have been either enormous or inconsequential, but this close contemporary of Erasmus (*Training in Dialectic* [1543] and *Rhetorica* [1548]) decisively called "rhetoric" the study of style and delivery, to separate it from logic. Logic included invention and arrangement, Ramus said, and always had. Ramus's division was in the service not of a philosophic position or of elegant variation but of a neat pedagogy. His schematic presentation of a universal system for teaching is often called the most prominent success that an otherwise diminishing rhetoric had, for it was widely influential, competitive with (if deferential to) Aristotelian rhetoric, and easily perceived to have caused rather than to have stood beside reasons for calling the subject of rhetoric "figuration."[5]

In seemingly very different moves, then, both Erasmus and Ramus also echoed and solidified the postclassical Augustinian position that training the whole orator is not the necessary center of rhetoric. Christian doctrines, not Cicero's or Quintilian's sociopolitical discourse study, could elsewhere create the morally worthy individual. Meanwhile, Ramus's complex pedagogic diagrams democratized rhetorical learning, transforming rhetoric to a visual field. He wrote rhetoric on paper, neither relying on the examples in anecdotes and in tributes to rhetors that classical rhetoricians had used nor stressing that personal successes and failures within communities of consequential persons can be imitated or avoided.

Renaissance theorists who wrote handbooks cataloguing the figures must, of course, be distinguished from later theorists who have visions of a closed, independent, self-referential world of writing. For them, metaphor, or tropology, can become self-impelled creative forces. Renaissance theorists were instead taken by the same curiosity about the fixed but then common text that the later Roman theorists like Quintilian had been in the first, soon lost, literary manuscript culture. The Renaissance cultural context for rhetoric included discoveries and rediscoveries of languages and philosophy, which required cultural norms for evaluating large quantities of writing by people who had never before been known, either in person or by reputation. In this context, rhetoric as stylistics became a system that could apply ancient conventions to new, visually available, relatively context-free words. Style was altered and refined under the imagined pressure of textual isolation, which was now brought on by renewed literary manuscript and new print cultures. The text might, that is, newly become Socrates' homeless bastard, so Renaissance rhetoricians focused on the effects that its style might have on its audiences—effects that could be frozen and duplicated in print.

Consequently, if we look for *a* rhetoric that described the "authorial literacy" treated earlier, we are disappointed. The movements in Renaissance rhetoric that are commonly described in its histories do combine to authorize and authenticate "authorship" in the sense of a mixture of oratorical and textual presence. But insofar as rhetoric could be seen as a fault of the ancients, a system of words to substitute for newly prominent authorial observation and insight, it did not have renewals except in the service of this authorship. Francis Bacon, for instance, would have stopped new interpretations of rhetoric even in stylistic or pedagogic versions.

Rather than restore classical ideas of rhetoric, Bacon also relocated them, this time in the effects of rhetorical discourse on "auditors," for whom necessary variations of any sort of case, either "scientific" or "civil," must be made. His revised rhetoric, which emphasized meaning rather than "mere words," also acknowledged a need that was directly related to the new variety and number of available discourses in his time. Conceiving rhetoric to be the art of shaping all communication, Bacon moved ahead of stylistic and Ramistic limitations on the field. He responded to new critical masses of Renaissance writing, demanding a new art of discourse, but not one that Aristotle or Quintilian would have recognized.

That is, he opposed their earlier categorical tradition, criticizing it for manipulating words, as syllogisms do, and for not discovering new facts. His comprehensive empiricism was evident in his definition of rhetoric as "*to apply Reason to Imagination* for the better moving of the will."[6] This view suited, as stylistics and Ramism could not, the novelty and scope of new discourse institutions that were established by the time he wrote *The Advancement of Learning* in 1603.

As it is increasingly common to acknowledge, the later period in which Blair, Campbell, and Whately wrote rhetorics marked a restoration of literacy in England after its Cromwellian and Restoration declines in the seventeenth century. Print had become not merely possible but so common that distinct groups of readers emerged who were even more distant from the sources of texts in "authors" or in social institutions. Rhetoric, certainly following faculty psychology in the period, focused on connecting the writer's mind to a newly imagined "reader" who concerned Blair and Campbell. It becomes a study of "communication," and fewer complaints (like Bacon's) were heard about the loss of its domain of memory. New social, and then "mass," literacy was not the fictional "universal" literacy we imagine to be current, but literatures and readerships did inexorably take on discrete identities within the incrementally complicated phenomenon of public discourse.[7]

Classical culture had a largely spoken literature (epic, poem, drama), as well as written histories (usually post-hoc fictionalizations of events and speeches) and vast quantities of public documents like funeral orations and victory speeches. But the fall of this culture and the dominance of primitive Christianity resulted in a relatively slow generic recuperation, speeded by printing and publishing. In England at least, new reading audiences in the eighteenth century took up philosophy (Bacon, Hobbes, Locke, Hume, Berkeley), the novel (Defoe, Fielding, Richardson, Smollett, Stern), periodicals (*Spectator, Adventurer, Rambler, Idler, Gentleman's Magazine*) and literally text-reflexive works like Johnson's *Dictionary, Lives of the Poets,* and Shakespeare criticism. Craftsman printers gradually were translated into "publishers." The idea that one might earn a living as a "writer" became possible, if only by economic extension of the model of the medieval craftsman's patron.[8]

Richard Whately, whose *Elements of Rhetoric* was published in 1828 but who is generally grouped with eighteenth-century rhetoricians, thought of his *Rhetoric* as a companion to his treatment of logic. His definition, one of those echoing Ramus's intent, defines " 'Argumentative Composition,' generally and exclusively; considering Rhetoric (in conformity with the very just and philosophic view of Aristotle) as an offshoot from Logic" (chap. 1).[9] But Whately's "off-shoot" would not, his text reveals, have grown unfertilized in the earth Bacon had dug around rhetoric and logic. That is, his treatment marks another division of the subject and a new era of paradoxical fragmentation and discontinuities that has continued to the present.

Eighteenth-century-and-later definitions and theories of rhetoric emphasize readers and the private writing and reading of a text. Whately attended to writing with uncommon self-consciousness:

> It is evident that in its primary signification, Rhetoric had reference to public *Speaking* alone, as its etymology implies. But as most of the rules for Speaking are of course applicable equally to Writing, an extension of the term naturally took place; and we find even Aristotle, the earliest systematic writer on the subject whose works have come down to us, including his Treatise rules for such compositions as were not intended to be publicly recited. . . .
>
> The invention of Printing, by extending the sphere of operation of the Writer, has of course contributed to the extension of those terms which, in their primary signification, had reference to Speaking alone. Many objects are now accomplished through the medium of the Press, which formerly came under the exclusive province of the Orator; and the qualifications requisite for success are so much the same in both cases, that we apply the term "Eloquent" as readily to a Writer as to a Speaker; though, etymologically considered, it could only belong to the latter. Indeed, "Eloquence" is often attributed even to such compositions,—e.g., Historical works—as have in view an object entirely different from any that could be proposed by an Orator. (*Elements of Rhetoric*, introduction)

Rhetoricians did not draw Whately's point so finely again until a century later, when writing became one of many competing media and not the handmaiden to speech that he and his predecessors conceived it to be. Earlier writers had announced their theories to be offspring conceived by earlier people, but Blair, Campbell, Whately, and even Alexander Bain were the first in this canonical series to refer to learning about rhetoric from others' clearly named *books*. Stabilized written texts had begun to have a life of their own, in the same period that the rhetorical domain of memory no longer evoked even nostalgia.

Alexander Bain allied himself with Blair, Campbell, and

Whately, but his pedagogical version of rhetoric clearly demonstrated that the creation of correct, not persuasive, texts was to become the essence of rhetorical applications in composition. Although Bain chronologically followed Witherspoon at Princeton in identifying four "modes" of discourse, he is given credit for these categories because of his different sense that they demonstrate the "faculties" and the popularity of his *English Composition and Rhetoric* (1869). Representing associationist psychology, he might be styled as the first behaviorist lexicographer of rhetoric, insofar as he looked at pedagogy from a more "objective" distance. The teacher, he said, can do little about "the pupils' fund of expression" in English and can be "a trainer" of the students' "discrimination between good and bad in expression" (preface).[10] Bain catalogues numbered precepts, stating rules that are (in view of what little could be done about the "fund of expression") descriptive rather than demonstrative. For example, his advice about the forensic discourse that naturally absorbed early rhetorics is not advice but imperative disclosure: "4.II Political Oratory. The pleader in criminal cases has to persuade a judge and jury to find an accused person guilty or innocent" (172).

Bain's textbook provides three sections: "Style in General" (treated very particularly), "Kinds of Composition," and "Oratory." He defined the latter as "the influencing of men's conduct and beliefs by spoken or written address" (171). In this transmitted tradition of explanations of rhetoric, his book was the first major rearrangement to locate contexts for speaking or writing *after* extensive particular advice about parts of discourse. "Writing" (treated as constructing sentences and then paragraphs) preceded persuading, "oratory."

If it appears that the sort of rhetoric Bain wrote had lost its "memory," becoming a set of lessons primarily about "writing" in the mode of Edmund Coote's lessons on reading and spelling (chap. 2), it is also true that rhetoric had added a specifically new domain to its categories. But this domain has been accorded even less honor in rhetorical studies than Bain's rules for writing sentences and paragraphs. "Elocution," originally meant to be "style," had been renewed and elaborated to mean lessons in reading aloud. This phenomenon has never been comfortably assimilated within rhetorical study, but we might see it as a normal development in a discipline that has persistently, as we have seen, relocated its emphases to accommodate the effects of written texts. The clarity with which this movement reveals the nature of written subjectivity makes it, ironically, our clearest precedent for establishing a field of written composition.

The elocutionary movement, begun in seventeenth-century works on preaching (e.g., John Wilkins's *Ecclesiastes, or A Discourse Concerning the Gift of Preaching, 1646*) and steadily present thereafter, became the embarrassingly popular eighteenth- and nineteenth-century addition to rhetorical study. Its most prominent examples were Thomas Sheridan's *Lectures on Elocution* (1765) and *Lectures on Reading* (1775), John Walker's *Elements of Elocution* (1781), and Gilbert Austin's *Chironomia or a Treatise on Rhetorical Delivery* (1806). Its popularity and survival until recently in American schools, and to this day in England, are ironic in the face of the original meaning of *elocution*, the *lexis* of schemes, tropes, and figures that are chosen to execute invention and arrangement. Modern elocution has instead been declamation, identified as *actio* and *pronuntiatio* in original rhetoric. It differed from them, however, for while Greek and Roman schoolchildren learned in these lessons literally how to pronounce the words that were recorded in graphically fragmented texts, later students were taught gestures and postures (pictured in detail, for example, in Sheridan) that would convey life to, and from, print.

Wilbur Samuel Howell's explanation of the rise of elocution has been the standard contentious interpretation of how this new thread was spun off from a fragmenting rhetorical skein:

> Only rhetorical pronunciation had remained free of attack during the period which Ramus had started by making delivery the second division of his bifurcated rhetoric and his opponents had ended by returning delivery to its former place in the scheme which included invention, arrangement, and style. The elocutionists in seeking to elevate the fifth part of rhetoric into a new prominence at least could have claimed that they were responding to the criticisms against the traditional system in such a way as to preserve only what that system itself had saved from successful assault. In other words, the basic justifi-

cation of their school could have been that the previous immunity of *pronuntiatio* to attack entitled it to be regarded as having a continuing validity.[11]

As Howell says, conceding defeat, "these practices came to stand in the public mind for the whole of rhetorical doctrine, and rhetoric came to mean empty and insincere speaking" (145). But, as we have seen, this series of amputations was not the origin of earlier public opinions of rhetoric, nor their only sustaining cause. Even from the point of view of insiders themselves to rhetoric, accepting Howell's interpretation is a logical contradiction. It belies the popularity of Erasmus, Ramus, and especially of Blair's *Lectures* and similar continuing modifications of newly and loosely "classical" rhetoric from Bacon through the present.

Those with a little distance on historical transmissions of rhetoric that emphasize its primarily oral and threatened disciplinary status as a remnant might more plausibly link elocution's new location of rhetoric literally *in* public speaking with the phenomenon of written texts. The popularity of elocution occurred not at its beginning (ca. 1646) but later, when readerships were better established. The movement was less a defensive, protective remnant of rhetoric, hiding in a conditional trench, than a positive and natural response to the need for reading aloud in public from works that the speaker had not written and had neither the time nor the training to memorize. Once writing became a socially and economically independent medium in the eighteenth century, readers needed lessons in fitting written words to speech from, as it were, the other direction. After dictionaries and custom standardized a "correct" pronunciation that was attached to phonemes rather than to fluid tone or dramatic emphasis, and no one had actually *heard* an author's voice or one like it, the art of delivery had to be given special attention. If I am "quoting" aloud— without this meaning that I am repeating what "Demosthenes" (or "this writer") actually "says" but instead quoting to re-create a listening experience from a text that may never have been spoken aloud—I need lessons in the conventions of this new situation. I in fact need new conventions for public reading. Elocution restored presence to a graphic text, where no original presence or evocative biography of an "author" was to be found. Its importance as a moment in the developing phenomenology of texts cannot be underestimated.

Howell offers reasons actually more in support of this view than of his own. He notes, for instance, that religious services had become "much more . . . readings from the Book of Common Prayer than . . . original preachings and exhortations" (154). Thomas Sheridan defended his teaching of elocution on these same grounds, saying that increased veneration of ancient literature and the concomitant fall of public and political action, and thus of oratory, are the same phenomenon. Sheridan blamed "men of the greatest abilities" for withdrawing to the contemplative (bookish) life, leaving the field of public speaking open to tyrants. He explained that this withdrawal affected language by separating its spoken from its written performances, making it an action through the eye. "It is generally thought that the one [speech or writing] is equally well calculated to answer the end as the other. . . . But . . . the noblest purposes of social communication, can not possibly be attained, by any language but that which proceeds from the living voice.[12] The consequences of placing writing over speech should, he says, give us pause.

We can similarly recall Samuel Johnson's guarded approval of Boswell's accent (Boswell had studied elocution with Sheridan) and imagine how many newly transplanted people were required to reconcile their geographic mobility against an increasing graphic linguistic stability in eighteenth-century England. The absence of elocution from most serious studies of what "rhetoric" has been exemplifies how rarely the subject is associated with *its* subject, actual discourse situations. The almost total disappearance of elocution now is further testimony to a new world in which writing has thoroughly replaced shaped public speech.

Ignoring elocution points to another absence in definitions contained in later treatments of rhetoric. They make remarkably few self-conscious references to the medium on which they rely. I. A. Richards, Kenneth Burke, Stephen Toulmin, and Chaim Perelman have by and large assumed that writing and speech may be addressed by the same discussion. But this assumption indicates that the theories of these writers also depend on writing and textual experience for their reconstructions of rhetoric. Theories following Bain have most often been composed to be read and not to be heard in lecture halls or public forums. But in their unspoken graphological assumptions, they define the problem that has kept us from emphasizing that rhetoric is about discourse situations—which are not now those of speech.

2   Rhetoric as Modern Writings: The Presence of the Text

We conceive of "modern" rhetorics as distinct from the lessons of Whately, Bain, and elocution, but we rarely notice that the distinction most relevant to our own concerns is that modern rhetorics are embedded in the written world and the problems of writers and readers even while they attempt to extend their work from ancient oral theories and practices. I. A. Richards, for instance, maintained a connection to Whately in his *Philosophy of Rhetoric* (1936). In this attempt to unravel the relation of speakers to their symbols, he might be styled the last of those writers whose address to literature and to rhetoric needed no self-conscious "placement" by a then-new literary profession. For him, pedagogical, literary, and rhetorical theories blended in a vision of the "rhetorical" problematic.

But even Richards's brief statement of an explicit definition of rhetoric shows how distinct a modern characterization of the subject would inevitably be: "Rhetoric, I shall urge, should be a study of misunderstanding and its remedies. We struggle all our days with misunderstandings, and no apology is required for any study which can prevent or remove them."[13]

Richards thought earlier associationist rhetorics were useless: "the applications of these theories in the detail of Rhetoric are their own refutation" (17). Their forerunners, "old Rhetoric," oppose his project, for the older study was "an offspring of dispute" (24). His new location of rhetoric is in words, but neither the "appropriate diction" of stylistic rhetoric nor the words-as-signs of ancient philosophy:

> Since the whole business of Rhetoric comes down to comparisons between the meanings of words, the first prob-

> lem, I think, should be this. How, if the meaning of a word is,
> in this sense, the missing parts of its contexts, how then should
> we compare the meanings of two words? (37)
>
> But where old Rhetoric treated ambiguity as a fault in
> language, and hoped to confine or eliminate it, the new Rheto-
> ric sees it as an inevitable consequence of the powers of lan-
> guage and as the indispensable means of most of our most
> important utterances—especially in Poetry and Religion. (40)

Richards might have been closer to the mark if he had said
that the "old Rhetoric" had hoped to confine or eliminate
ambiguity by perfecting a rhetor's appropriate choices of
words. In any case, the "powers of language" Richards wants
to explain clearly are written, textual powers. Richards's location of rhetoric in the study of words and his attention to their
ambiguities relative to "contexts" reveal his assumption that
communication will be done in writing and, more important,
through writing. But the novelty of "neutral exposition," which
he pointedly distinguishes as a discourse mode, shows that
Richards did not think of writing as an entirely independent
medium that could submerge the personal intentions of a
writer. "Of course ambiguities are a nuisance in exposition as,
in spite of my efforts, you have certainly been feeling. But
neutral exposition is a very special limited use of language,
comparatively a late development to which we have not (outside some parts of the sciences) yet adapted it" (40). Considering that Richards wrote this some decades after the first college-level courses in expository writing were instituted in
America, we can see how explicit, not symbolic or general,
their teaching was meant to be.

Richards's anecdote about inventions of new words
that were being coined for science reinforces this statement. It
shows him intrigued by the same reversal of priorities between
writing and speech that Sheridan had seen as justifications for
the elocutionary movement. Richards quotes Sir John Murray
on his experience as he included new coinages in the *Oxford
English Dictionary*. When Murray would ask a word's intro-
ducer about its pronunciation, he would get no help: "The
answer received was 'that he has never thought of its pronunciation, does not presume to say how it ought to be pro-

nounced, and leaves it to people to pronounce as they like, or to the DICTIONARY to say what is the *right* pronunciation.' This, Sir James complained, inverts the established order by which speech comes first" (76–77), an inversion that actually describes historical rhetoric.

After Richards's compression of rhetoric into "words," Kenneth Burke's definitions of the subject on which he founded his literary studies are significant for their extensiveness among definitions that show a changing relation to writing. Rhetoric has a "range," he says, not a point of being. He placed and replaced the term in many settings:

> The *Rhetoric* [Aristotle's] deals with the possibilities of classification in its partisan aspects; it considers the ways in which individuals are at odds with one another, or become identified with groups more or less at odds with one another.[14]
>
> Rhetoric is concerned with the state of Babel after the Fall. Its contribution to a "sociology of knowledge" must often carry us far into the lugubrious regions of malice and the lie. (23)
>
> Classical rhetoric stresses the element of explicit design in rhetorical enterprise. But one can systematically extend the range of rhetoric, if one studies the persuasiveness of false or inadequate terms which may not be directly imposed upon ourselves, in varying degrees of deliberateness and awareness, through motives indeterminately self-protective and/or suicidal. (35)
>
> We come upon another aspect of Rhetoric: its nature as *addressed*, since persuasion implies an audience. A man can be his own audience, in so far as he, even in his secret thoughts, cultivates certain ideas or images for the effect he hopes they may have upon him; he is here what Mead would call "an 'I' addressing its 'me' " and in this respect he is being rhetorical. (38)
>
> Now, the basic function of rhetoric, the use of words by human agents to form attitudes or to induce actions in other human agents, is certainly not "magical." (411)
>
> If we then begin by treating this *erroneous* and *derived* magical use as *primary*, we are invited to treat a *proper* use of language (for instance, political persuasion) simply as a vestige of benightedly prescientific magic. (242)
>
> *For rhetoric as such is not rooted in any past condition of*

human society. It is rooted in an essential function of language itself,
a function that is wholly realistic, and is continually born anew; the
use of language as a symbolic means of inducing cooperation in beings
that by nature respond to symbols. (43)

Burke's work is infrequently self-conscious about the scene of writing itself, but it nonetheless measures the distance rhetoric has come in its relation to particular discourse situations. He notes how powerful Hitler believed the spoken, as opposed to written, words to be[15] and asserts that *"the reading of a book on the attaining of success is in itself the symbolic attaining of that success"* (298). In this statement, writing has become the world that absorbs personal presence and enacts the "reality" that Burke so often relates to rhetoric's purposes.

But Burke's rhetoric takes place largely in and through writing. Literature encompasses "rhetoric," not the reverse. He only indirectly modifies rhetorical theory to acknowledge writing, stating that modern journalism calls for a new *topic,* in Aristotle's sense of common locales for finding something to say. He says that contemporary discourse situations have created a new "level of 'reality' " to which rhetoric might adapt by cataloging "a kind of *timely topic,* such as that of the satirical cartoon, which exploits commonplaces of a transitory nature." This transitoriness is not due to the isolated or ephemeral nature of the cartoon genre but occurs because "they are *more persuasive* with people living under one particular set of circumstances."[16] Burke points out, for instance, that a cartoon about unemployment would have a hard time getting published in a time of prosperity. He proposes to examine his new *topic* in relation to cartoons in the *New Yorker.*

This apparently offhand suggestion in Burke exemplifies how central the locales of discourse are to rhetorical theory, even when they are only implicitly recognized. Printing, publishing, and inexpensive paper create writing that finally is impermanent, not "a record" but so ephemeral that it has become, even in public forms, as transitory as local speech. Time—or "timely"—can be conceived to be "the audience" for writing, disembodied but nonetheless that to which the "speech," in precedent oratorical rhetoric, must be adapted. Burke's work is the first modern treatment of "rhetoric" that assumes significant discourse is unapologetically, and unconditionally, "written" in the most comprehensive sense of the word.

Changes that move rhetoric from person to set speech and also to the elements of texts finally, of course, locate rhetoric in the reader. Chaim Perelman, whose internationally influential *New Rhetoric* (written with L. Olbrechts-Tyteca [1958]) limits rhetoric to argument, emphasizes "that it is in terms of an audience that argument develops."[17]

In Perelman's renovated traditional view, the conditions for discourse must be explicitly addressed so that writing will not be treated as distinct from oratory. He explains that rhetoric is no longer a matter of "speaking well." His justification of the "application" of rhetoric to writing is a subtext in most contemporary theories in the speech-communication tradition: "The result of our emphasis on written texts, since these latter occur in the most varied forms, is that our study is conceived *with complete generality* [my italics]; it will not be confined to discourses considered as an entity of more or less conventionally admitted structure and length" (6). He says further that he will preserve from traditional rhetoric "the audience," whose existence is evoked by mentioning a speech. We forget, he says, that writing is also always addressed to an audience. But "the physical absence of his readers can lead a writer to believe that he is alone in the world, though his text is always conditioned . . . by those persons he wishes to address" (7).

Perelman is perhaps too conciliatory with oral rhetoric in this overview, for his major contribution is the concept of the "universal audience" that in fact depends on writers and readers to be participants in his vision of argumentation. His theory depends entirely on replacing our sense of rhetorical immediacy with a new perception of actions among significant writings and the institutions that render them consequential. Nonetheless, when he and Olbrechts-Tyteca address "presence," they suppress the issue of specific textual interactions. Their fairly extensive treatment of problems of bringing to mind "what is actually absent but what is considered important" (117) in persuasion explores only the psychological situation of the speaker, who may use onomatopoeia or repetition as "figures of presence" (174). Neither do they mention the increased distance, or absence, of both speaker *and* various argumentative points that writing necessitates, nor do they connect writing at all to the issue of bringing important issues into presence. This detailed consideration of persuading the universal audience to seize on or ignore various issues over-looks the actual space that the audience now occupies. These new rhetoricians have so entirely relocated the problem of writing, which Plato considered in the *Phaedrus*, that their argumentation is also "alone in the world," disembodied and without its particular material presence.

Stephen Toulmin, a philosopher, has also contributed to treatments of contemporary rhetoric as argumentation, but through its relation to logic rather than to Perelman's choice of audience analysis. In *The Uses of Argument* (1958), he says that argument is a movement from accepted "data," from a "warrant" to a "claim." His *Human Understanding, I* (1972), on the other hand, places him firmly in the camp of broader rhetorical theory, although it does not explicitly explain "rhetoric."

In the later study, where Toulmin analyzes the organi-zation and evolution of intellectual professions and disci-plines, he shows how far removed ideas of an "individual" are from their influential manifestations in specific institutions. Persuasiveness, he says, now depends on speaking " 'for and in the name of' the science concerned."[18] Individual opinion has become institutionalized, at least in academic professions, so that "an authority" has become "an authoritative view . . . both in the disciplinary sense, i.e., the view supported by the best accredited body of experience and in the professional sense, i.e., the view supported by the influential authorities in the subject" (264). Influential authorities become so, he says, by successfully participating in the collective project of a discipline and profession and by having good timing.

Placing the collective voice where Perelman locates the universal audience, Toulmin examines another consequence of the modern disciplinary borders that result from concatena-tions of texts. He depicts disciplines as communities of speak-ers or writers, whose *ethos* is fed by, but transcends, individu-als. In a post-Cartesian age, he thus reinvents medieval textual literacy as another product of mixed oral-literate interactions.

Juxtaposed against Perelman's approach, Toulmin's analysis completes a picture of writing-to-writing (rather than speaker-to-audience) rhetorical theory. Ancient "speaker" and "audience" are finally, in these new terms, "discourse" and "readership." These two elements interact "politically," page by page.

These modern definitions of rhetoric by its insiders sustain the persistent form—deference to authority followed by objections to that authority—that significantly illuminates the changes they record. That is, changes in rhetoric appear to present a persistent tension between stable, authoritative, and ultimately repressive codification and *practice*—which is unstable, uncertain, and, in its best aspects, creative. Almost any new definition of rhetoric hallows the authority of Aristotle, Cicero, and Quintilian and thus also preserves traces of "attacks" by Plato, Socrates, or, in his particular manner, Augustine. But new definitions also always assert the ephemeral and provisional appropriateness of rhetoric. Kenneth Burke, for instance, as Daniel Fogarty reports, has been "really" interested in "the achievement of peace."[19] Burke's analysis of Hitler was no flat "rhetorical analysis," but vital, a response to an immediate threat.

The sense of immediate urgency exemplified there implicitly pervades Augustine's Christian version of rhetoric, Bacon's new empiricist treatment, and most renovations that begin by asserting or negating alternative contexts for their new views of rhetoric. Each new beginning contains overtones of relocation, renovation, reclamation, and experimentation for the not entirely lost subject. Rhetoric—always "addressed" rather than even provisionally capable of isolation from its own practices—is an art of "presence" in all the senses that word comprehends. Each new definition is a new moment, not part of a traditional historical scene.

What is most important for us to note is how each of these renovations of rhetoric commands a place as perpetrator and modifier within a sequence of written words. Rhetoric's definition(s) not only *are* but also *re-present* writing, for these definitions have their increasingly material settings in their moves from lecture to book. In this light, definitions of rhetoric change their answers to the question, "What is the art of discourse?" not because a philosophy around them has changed, but because discourse and discourse situations are the fabric of philosophy. As in Saussure's analogy of the relation of language paradigms to utterances in language, cutting through one side of a page results in cutting through the other. Institutionalized "thought" and discourse are not necessarily identical, but a rupture in one is a rupture in the other. Rhetoric cannot be accurately understood outside this context, discoursing itself.

This is not a new idea, as Michel Foucault's analyses of power and discourse relations have shown. But in the case of rhetoric, the art/science of discourse itself, such analyses have been uncommon. The definitions reviewed here to exemplify change have rarely been examined to show their participation in always reemerging disciplinary presence or in connections between this discipline and changes in the powers attributed to speaker or utterance or audience. These three specifically rhetorical *topoi*—the credibility of a discipline, its assumptions about presence, and the relation of the two—vary in prominence according to their discourse "scene." They create not Burke's five elements of dramatic ratios for analyzing texts but a complex calculus in redundant and discontinuous cultural time. As I have argued throughout this account, understanding rhetorical history involves explaining these power relations in terms of textual, not oral, institutions. The importance of writing for the art of speaking can be verified in the ways that these definitions within the field are persistently nostalgic. They repeatedly long for unity among these *topoi*, especially a unity placed in the person of the orator, in a lost predominantly oral world, whose traces many still give priority in basic conceptions and teachings about discourse.

This chronology of prominent redefinitions of rhetoric shows most clearly that rhetorical theory has slowly invented for itself another world entirely, where multiple and diverse texts are a lively universe of inscriptions, which interact as vividly as the characters of good men speaking. Definitions of rhetoric from within the field imply that rhetorical theories at any particular time need specification. These specifications can highlight ruptures in the side of the paper that they have tended to ignore, discourse institutions that rhetoric cannot describe, or change, without being changed itself.

5 The Educational Result

Rhetoric and Composition

I have proposed a textual rhetoric in this study as a possible way to relate the concerns of composition and rhetorical studies in the contexts that contemporary theory and a history of writing provide. This proposal is based not on customary traditions about historical continuity between rhetoric and composition instruction but on placing writing and writers in a position of agency in a history and theory of discourse. Although this position of agency obviously does not require specific applications of textual rhetoric to writing pedagogy or research, it does offer some ways to look at composition instruction in higher education as a historically grounded phenomenon, the logical cultural product of changes in conditions for producing discourse. This distinct discipline might theorize its object of study, the act of writing, in terms of this relevant history. Textual rhetoric offers, that is, a comprehensive way to describe specifically textual activities. It suggests ways to account for a piece of writing as the result of, and as a contribution to, both cultural and textual histories beyond the immediate "rhetorical situation" that is usually invoked for guidance when an act of writing is equated with an oral performance.

A writer now shares the situation that Plato once imagined for the written text and used to characterize the dangers of rhetoric. A writer's action cannot be linked to his or her fixed personality or to unified "character" in the writer. The writer cannot represent "pure" meaning, of whatever quality, because written language necessarily will capture the writer's first intentions and invoke a distant and unknown reader's textual experiences. Consequently, the act of writing is a process that fictionalizes stability, requiring that the writer will be judged according to his or her awareness of the possible fictions within textual worlds. A virtuoso performance in writing thus takes place within cultural, textual, situational, and graphic conventions that textual rhetoric addresses. The writer may allow any of these considerations to stimulate and to constrain the text, whose future revision will be inevitable. And this writer nonetheless writes as if writing can make an assertion or place an equally fictionalized personal presence within written words.

I have assumed that working out this theory of writers historically, philosophically, and in terms of definitions of rhetoric will contribute to ongoing reconceptualizations within composition studies because I take the act of writing to be still somewhat hidden in the persistent convention that writing only "contains" individual speech or thought. Most theorists and teachers of written composition still unquestioningly emphasize a direct connection between thought and spoken-to-written language. Many lament the difference between "authors" and the halting textual voices of imitative ("insincere" or "inauthentic") student writing. They aim to produce "student writers" who write and read "for themselves," assuming that a thesis may be "stated" with discernible clarity, coherence, and completeness. Composition, more than any other textual study, necessarily confronts writing as discovery, as play, and as process because it faces unstable student texts that have been written by those who seem to know only their own oral culture. But common practices in the field persistently honor oppositions to discovery, play, and process: product, seriousness, and perfect communication. Even the most enlightened often relegate the instabilities of writing to "pedagogy" while retaining in their descriptions of "rhetoric" an ideal of assertive and stable texts.

Alternatives to these tacit assumptions and their results depend on reconceiving both student writers and the act of writing. This process is already under way in composition studies' new emphasis on contextual pedagogy and research, and it may be clarified by looking briefly at three manifestations of "the writer" I have theorized and historically described. The first is from early American rhetorical pedagogy, in which Ellery T. Channing offered a manifesto for moving American composition instruction away from oratory and into the less determinate discourse of writing. The second is a picture of the student writer, who is a product of this manifesto and other pre twentieth-century social and educational changes. The third, the construction of the "basic writer" in Mina Shaughnessy's *Errors and Expectations* will, I hope, explain and generalize the situation any contemporary writer faces. Each of these instances can help to focus the now problematic relation between composition instruction and oral rhetoric.

1   A Relocated American Rhetoric

Few members of any branch of textual studies have clear ideas about the purposes or origins of specific courses to teach writing, or of the relation of these courses to an earlier teaching of rhetoric. There are particularly good reasons why this is so. Only in the last century, primarily in America, has writing been taught discretely and self-consciously in higher education, or has this teaching been accompanied by serious research. The novelty of this study, despite attempts to equate it with continuing pedagogies from rhetoric, has raised a new set of practical difficulties that have postponed the desire to integrate composition into its own unacknowledged theoretical contexts. Meanwhile, the new profession of composition has been reputedly even more questionable than the itinerant early Sophists' work. Its bases in inevitable results from the cultural fact of writing have not been clarified. Usually, opinions of composition teaching or of its disciplinary status are backed only by a ceremonial morality of faint praise. Composition shares the status, and the difficulties, that surround other quite different but equally populist academic studies.

To say that writing has only recently been taught or become the subject for academic research invites immediate contradiction, even though the novelty of its professions and publications is obvious.[1] But it is equally obvious that neither writing nor reading is learned without formal lessons and that Western education has included many sorts of writing instruction from its beginning. People have undertaken composition—"for themselves" and not just to record or copy—for centuries. The issue is, then, how written composition became a discrete study that applies to a new, precisely discrete presence in texts. This question is not merely academic or pedagogic, for the new student of writing has a relation to all written texts; this particular student tells us a great deal about both textual theory and history.

As we saw earlier, cultures based on vernacular writing developed well ahead of specific education *for* widely participatory vernacular writing.[2] Although rhetorical pedagogy is intimately intertwined with practice and with practical effects in discourse, it has always been conservative. Even well after general education for local children became an acknowledged responsibility of governments rather than of benevolent estate owners or parishes, lessons in discourse were formed to equip children of whatever class with the same sort of oratorical training that Elyot had outlined for rulers in *The Book of the Governor*. While the invention of print very slowly began to imply that a citizen would write rather than speak, rhetorical education never self-consciously separated spoken from written relations to a "text." Nor did it assume that students would write specifically vernacular prose, even when they took up the bardic, local voices of the writing poets who were addressed in Renaissance literary apologies.[3] One reason that Alexander Bain's *English Composition and Rhetoric* (1869) so quickly captured the pedagogic imagination of schoolteachers was that it was among the first specifically *English* treatments of discretely taught writing.

But even in its time, Bain's vernacular pedagogy did not absolutely describe actual teaching practices in most schools. Students translated from Latin to English and the reverse to learn "to write" through the early twentieth century. The difference between becoming educated for public life, which meant for public speaking or for oratorically patterned writing in local situations, and becoming educated for more limited and practical written composition was determined, as I described earlier, by the curricular year that members of discrete classes left school.

Consequently, specifically tracing the advanced student *writer* and various ways of learning to write has not until recently interested historians of rhetorical, literary, or even literacy, education. Humanistic education in texts has been thought of as an education in reading them, not in writing them. As Furet and Ozouf summarize in *Reading and Writing: Literacy in France from Calvin to Jules Ferry*:

> We are inclined to forget today, that for a long time writing was really a technical exercise, involving instruments, muscular gymnastics and a knack. Jean Meyer rightly reminds us that although we now think of reading and writing as two elementary and simultaneous learning processes, they used to be culturally dissociated skills, and that historically speaking there were at least two types of written civilization, those governed by the scribe, in which writing was queen, and those of the *literati*, in which it was no more than manual labor. Like the rest of ancient Europe, France was in an ambiguous situation in this respect. . . . Reading's original necessity—the ability to read the word of God—meant that it kept its claims to universality. It was an instrument of salvation, whereas writing ceased to be an art, to become a convenience.[4]

But even in histories of composition itself, which have avoided ending with the logic of textual rhetoric, writing instruction has often been assumed to be chronicled by educational practices that were meant to guide speaking. Edward P. J. Corbett, for instance, identifies the history of rhetorical education, and by implication the history of composition instruction, with the history of rhetorics that were frequently used as textbooks in England and America.[5] He thereby implicitly suggests that learning public speaking and learning public writing have consistently been equivalent ventures, which is not, as we have seen, precisely the case.

If we could separate good textual theory from good textual pedagogy, there would be no problem with taking this textbook perspective on the history of writing instruction even now. Practices in discourse education generally have integrated reading, speaking, and one or another version of writing. Most people dedicated to humanistic ideas about what it means to be able to write still associate this ability with having read a canon, not with having been schooled specifically to publicize one's own ideas. A traditional mixture of reading, writing, and speaking was fostered in even the most apparently specialized Renaissance stylistic textbooks like Erasmus's *De Copia*, which would have allowed a schoolmaster to teach all three processes, given some elaborate extensions of "style" to "idea."[6] The "writing" in primary-level Renaissance and later textbooks (which were often used after secondary education for undergraduates)[7] was primarily basics for citizen-readers. Yet, the practices of keeping commonplace books and of writing exercises for recitation guaranteed that students would link composing for public speech with writing, at least if they received a complete curriculum. As late as 1906, Charles Sears Baldwin's textbook, *Composition: Oral and Written*, gave equal treatment to oratorical and to written composition.

In any of the historical pedagogies from ancient to modern times, the specific purpose of either practice writing or practice speaking was to learn the conventions of public discourse. The student was first educated to use writing to record "himself"—to sign papers and copy moral passages. Later, the student learned to read great authors and to use writing to respond to or copy this reading. Writing was practiced at this stage as a pedagogically (rather than institutionally) framed sort of textual literacy, in which the students' writing acknowledged and preserved canonical texts.

In America, however, advanced students began in the nineteenth century to learn a rhetoric that would serve the cause of secondary, "authorial" literacy. Distinctly American needs relocated the traditional focus of rhetorical education for upper-class university students on shaping independent spoken discourse. In America, the pressure to unite an international collection of citizens under common documents rather than in widely divergent orally transmitted customs produced a divergent set of practices and theories. They assert that "writing" is not a supplement to the presence of the person or to an imagined voice.

This study has already described other movements from oral to written locales for authorial presence. Rhetorical theories and handbooks since the Renaissance have recognized both writing and readers, as elocutionary texts, Whately's introduction to the *Elements of Rhetoric*, Richards' *Philosophy of Rhetoric*, and Perelman's *New Rhetoric* all show. But this pointed history of appearances of writing in changing rhetorical theory may also be found in advanced discourse

education in America. At first, colonial America transported
the received Ramian version of classical rhetoric that was current in seventeenth-century England.[8] Students at Harvard,
for instance, were more strictly prohibited from speaking English than those at Oxford and Cambridge.[9] Neither educated
speech nor its writing was vernacular, so discourse education—and educational discourse—were classical imitations.
They omitted contemporary examples that involved publicly
or politically immediate situations. Although the students in
seventeenth- and eighteenth-century American colleges were
deeply committed to practicing and participating in public
debate (Halloran 260), the curriculum stayed narrowly formal
and narrowly Ramian for some time.

But the best accounts we have of early American rhetoric indicate that innovative strains of distinctly American doctrines were soon mixed in the progress of merely transported
English and Scottish rhetoric. In particular, John Witherspoon,
who had been educated in Scotland and who lectured as
president of Princeton between 1768 and 1794, strongly believed that orators might be made by systematic training and
individual application. His lectures transmitted a rhetoric that
was more comprehensive than Ramian rhetoric, although he
valued "selecting what is proper" to include in a composition
over "inventing what is tolerable."[10] He treated invention
much more slightly than Aristotle had. Witherspoon also, as
would have been natural in one so far from his own educational home, established portable written sources as the best
places for students to find material to imitate. He outlined
four aims of discourse (information, demonstration, persuasion, and entertainment) and, in the process, casually equated
written with oral discourse.

For Witherspoon as well as for John Quincy Adams and
Ellery T. Channing, the first holders of the Boylston Chair of
Rhetoric at Harvard, references to writing have more to do
with eighteenth-century belletristic rhetoric and its movement
from oral to literary categories than they do with the students'
own multiple purposes for writing.[11] The Board of Overseers'
legislation establishing this chair explicitly listed its holders'
duties, which included the direction to "inspect and correct
their [the students'] written translations of elegant passages

of Latin and Greek assigned by him for that purpose; and in the latter part of the year, specimens of their own compositions as their progress in letters may permit" (Guthrie, 4:101).

Elephalet Pearson, who had framed these directions, seems to have been influenced by John Ward, who had lectured at Gresham College between 1720 and 1758 and who had asserted that "since the rules for speaking and writing are the same [i.e., when the formation of sentences is being considered], under speaking we are to include writing, and each art [rhetoric and grammar] is to be considered as treating of both."[12] As Wallace Douglas has pointed out, this reasoning by Ward through Pearson about these interchangeable rules rested easily in the popularity of stylistic exercises from the sixteenth century on. Teachers could accomplish "enforcement" by assigning lists of schemes and tropes for memorization and then require the Latin theme to be developed in light of one set of formal terms one time and later by another set (107).

Each holder of the Boylston Chair, from Adams to Archibald MacLeish and after, redefined these statutes in practice. Channing's students wrote themes fortnightly, responding to a generally unrecognized achievement by Channing, opening the door to popularized and vernacular, rather than purely public and classical, college-level writing instruction. Channing's lectures (1819–51) quite clearly define the American transition from oratory to composition as an ideal. He in fact emphasized how important it was to relinquish spoken power in favor of distinctly written presence and individual authority:

> The orator, the commander, his elevation and fall, these are the important incidents and personages that are constantly thrust upon our notice; we are always looking at a few prominent men and their extraordinary deeds. But when you look at society now, you see everywhere a disposition to place the security of nations and of every individual on the broad foundation of laws and institutions, and to make it the interest of the highest as well as humblest citizen to respect in them.[13]

This rhetorical manifesto to communize discourse continues by placing writing ahead of speech:

> And what has been the effect of this state of things upon the orator . . . ?
>
> His consideration and power are not diminished merely because society is now under better regulation and more perfect security than it was formerly. The general diffusion of knowledge has had the same effect. We have now many other and more quiet ways of forming and expressing public sentiment, than public discussion in popular assemblies. Opinions are constantly coming to us from other men and all parts of the world, through many channels, and we are thus enabled to instruct ourselves, and to think liberally and independently on all subjects, and especially on the opinions that are most current at home, and which the ancient orator might have appealed to with unresisted and terrible power. (16–17)

This lecture, given at Channing's induction ceremony in 1819, announced premises that do not merely transfer rhetorical to writing instruction by slow slippage between traditions and new politics or technologies. In a distinction whose effects are still visible in the distinctness of American instructional basics in colleges, Channing actively asserted the superiority of diffused discourse powers, suggesting that a state should have many independent, individual heads rather than "a head" or an originating structure of Truth. With the faculty psychologists, he believed that education can improve not only a student's store of knowledge but his individual powers of mind. The function of the teacher is to promote "a ready command of all faculties and strengthen them to the utmost" (39).

Later, lecturing on "A Writer's Preparation," Channing stressed that reading should not supply students with their ideas nor make them "stop at what we read, to acquiesce in opinions, and take pride in calling men master. The only question is, do books make us less independent, less ourselves, than any other source of knowledge or exhilaration?" (193). As Wallace Douglas has said, "having in his first chapters described a rhetoric that had social and practical value because of its tie to written, published communication, Channing now was asserting a similar value for the school subject of composition" (118).

Channing explained writing as an internal, private process. He emphasized the individuality and self-generated power of writing in terms that markedly differ from earlier comments on composing as a matter of memory, form, and imitation:

> There is something worth our notice in the state of our minds when writing or when previously meditating upon our subject. . . . I can recognize certain habits and methods which I generally follow and which I know that I formed for myself. . . . The mind's perpetual activity and flow of thought are not dependent upon his will. . . . But we may compare our student to a man who has a river running through his ground, which divides into a multitude of channels. . . . The water runs by its own strength without any impulse from the man, and, whatever he does to it, will find a vent somewhere or other. He may turn, alter or direct its motion, but neither gave nor can take it away. So it is with our thoughts.
>
> It remains for every writer to say whether this representation is according to his experience. How much does he set down which he anticipated when he began to reflect upon a subject? After his work is done, how much does he find to be the result of previous design? He may begin with a prominent idea, which it is his purpose to lay open.
>
> Very soon unexpected relations spring up and gather round it, till sometimes the original subject becomes subordinate. (188–91)

These statements are worth quoting because they may well be the first preserved, explicitly rhetorical instructions that say writing is as close to thought as speech is, or that identify the particulars of a "maker's" processes in secondary literacy. Channing (quoting "Tucker's 'Light of Nature Pursued' ") associates student writing with the flowing but unpredictable composition that Coleridge described in the preface and text of "Kubla Khan." The student writer is thus potentially endowed with the same creative processes that an author has and is still always perceived to be pursuing the development of "both the moral and intellectual character."

Channing claimed to be ignorant of how students become writers, but his statements in this regard do not merely reflect typical antipathy to teaching "genius."[14] He says that he cannot account for how anyone *has* learned to write, but that "various, gradual and harmonious" instruction from grammar, rhetoric, dictionaries, reading, and lecture do indeed transform the poor beginner over time (185–86). He also says that learning and practicing writing are valuable in themselves, leading to the discourse independence of each student. Writing is appropriately particularized study.

2   The Student Writer

The implications of Channing's manifesto for the creation of a distinct student literacy deserve careful attention. Channing's *Lectures* contributed to a decline in spoken oratory whose signs were already plentiful. By 1794, a debate at Princeton had addressed "Whether debating or composition be more improving."[15] Although written examinations were not introduced as the method of evaluating students until the nineteenth century, written copies of the students' oral speeches had been submitted and examined long before. As Michael Halloran has explained in "Rhetoric in the American College Curriculum: The Decline of Public Discourse," this movement from spoken to written *status* for the student's identity was slow. "Composition" in the debate could have meant writing in preparation for speaking, not composition in writing for its own sake, and the "uses" may have been formal versus extemporaneous debate (254).

Early writing assignments were not our assignments to present "research" or to record private experiences but were very much like the rhetorical theses in support of one and another public issue that Ralph Johnson had required. Channing's theme topics, for instance, included "Stability of Literary Fame," "Describe the kind of character of Orations which may be properly called a part of Literature. Name some of the Eminent Orator-Authors," "Your idea of a nation's being independent—also of an individual's," and "Comparative difficulties of abolishing war, slavery, intemperance, etc."[16] Students were not, at least not at the advanced undergraduate level, asked about their summer vacations.

Nonetheless, by newly equalizing written and spoken discourse instruction and by examining students in writing, American higher education, which eventually abandoned the tutorial system and face-to-face discussion as primary ways to know students, moved away from these public writing assignments. It made a private communication between teacher and student the space that student discourse inhabits, at least in courses designed nominally to teach writing. Halloran notes that "communication anxiety" does not seem to have troubled eighteenth-century students, who so enjoyed public speaking that they formed literary and debate societies for vernacular exchanges (255). But the later growth of an equally troubling anxiety reflects not only our declining public surety but the rise of school writing and its artificial privacy. Such anxiety may have grown or become overt because students have over time been encouraged to perceive their "communication" as dualistically private and public. They must, in most academic settings, write what only a teacher reads, but they have often been assigned a task of imitating traditional public, persuasive forms of writing. Consequently, they may well have developed instead "audience/reader conflict" because they are asked to shout in the study, to whisper in the Coliseum.

Channing's contributions and the intrinsic privacy of student writing that is not associated with recitation were not the only pressures that created a new student writer, who writes for the sake of writing well rather than for oratorical practice. As Channing's theme topics show, *belletristic* rhetoric as Blair and Campbell had outlined it came to guide the subjects of school assignments. Public, political, moral concerns were adumbrated by questions about aesthetic literary judgments and analysis. Literature, in this renovated rhetorical curriculum, became more central. It began to be neither a source of commonplaces that all educated people could marshal to support their cases on the authority of ancient authors nor a source for traditional moral messages and exemplary styles. New aesthetic and self-referential studies of literature, evident in Channing's practices and in those of prominent successors to the Boylston Chair like Francis Child (1851–76), also—if inadvertently—encouraged student writers to take their own texts to be aesthetic products. Students came to value their "own style" or singular treatments of a subject on the grounds of the personal "originality" that Channing had outlined.[17] New American discourse instruction thereby paradoxically accomplished a division of literary from rhetorical

views of purpose, a separation that had not been effected over
the course of two thousand years of rhetorical history. This
separation became even more entrenched later, when "pure"
composition at the freshman level was instituted in ca. 1885,
and writing for any specific purpose was postponed to later
courses in separated literary and rhetorical curricula.

Additionally, the academic institutions that students
write within began to promote practical studies of science, technology, and agriculture in programs designed for vocational
advancement rather than for political or religious service to the
community. When the Morill Act (1862) established land-grant
universities in America, what had been theoretically diverse
aims of discourse in the doctrines of Witherspoon, Samuel
Newman, or Bain became applied methods for new "technical"
or I. A. Richards's purely "expository" writing. The division
between "literary" and "practical" writing was also thereby institutionalized, giving less and less importance to "rhetorical"
or "oratorical" writing for the public good. Writing, in addition
to developing each student's faculties of mind, became analogous to a career skill like "analysis," "criticism," or "management." It was a new kind of personal equipment. At even its
most advanced stages, it could be thought of as a "skill," if one
more complex than handwriting, spelling, or the grammatical
correctness that it had always encompassed. As a personal endowment taking the place of earlier training in polite and public
conversation and speechmaking, being able to write correctly in
prescribed forms became at least potentially a mark of a student
writer's independence from immediate social communities.

The student's sense of the broad social participation at
oratory's roots was further diminished by curricular specializa-
tion in the last part of the nineteenth century. Divisions of the
disciplines, which had begun with eighteenth-century specialized appointments to university chairs, also required that students write rather than recite or debate about general topics.
Also contributing were German ideals of specialized scholarship, in which learning is valued for its own sake, and the
elective system that quickly spread in the mid-to-late nineteenth century. All of these new academic systems furthered
the slow fragmentation of the community of scholars who
might all usefully attend a student's final (oral) examinations.

These changes revitalized a sort of scholasticism, or textual literacy, in educational institutions. Writing conventional texts became a mark of entering, as well as of transmitting or debating within, particular textualities defined by the disciplines and professions that Stephen Toulmin described as power relations in his new definition of rhetoric. As a result of these forces, which had never been intended to promote student writing, a new sort of literacy became a prerequisite for academic success. Whereas students had formerly been groomed to influence the public as ministers, politicians, or masters of polite learning, they were now required to join communities of specialists whose lexicon and research methods vary widely.

The particular relation of new student writers in this new context to primary, textual, and secondary literacies warrants further exploration. The new identity of the student writer that has been constructed from all these theoretical, practical, and institutional changes is decidedly not coequal to the student who had always learned to make letters, parse sentences, copy and imitate *sententia*, or write a clear hand. That writer and that writing have always been embedded in rhetorical and textual education, as they still are. "Mechanics," "grammar," and "well-organized paragraphs" have always certified writing as a preliminary to higher learning. That writer was, ideologically at least, required to show that he (the precise pronoun) had read "everything," the best that had been thought and said, and what had pleased many and pleased long. This ideal has had currency, since the documents stating its intents could be printed and widely dispersed.

But the student writer being taught to compose actually *in* writing, who is generally addressed with guarded mixtures of pathetic regret and irritation, has a new and currently generalized identity. His and her particular literacy participates in an intriguing double bind that is in large measure a result of the cultural facts of writing, print, and publishing. On the one hand, the student writer is thought to have been passed over for dispersals of unteachable "genius," the extenuated inheritance from Sidney to romantic and from practical economic creations of the gifted and inspired author. Nonetheless, the student writer is responsible for writing complexly rather than explaining or discussing ideas "in person," and is expected to be somehow original in this writing as well.

The student writer's presence, or persuasiveness, oscillates between the fundamentally oral culture of the classroom in educational institutions and the primarily written cultures of educational disciplines.[18] As a *student*, this writer appropriately points out, but does not personally assert, positions within already well established discourse communities. But as a *writer*, this student must by writing also assert and be accountable for at least a learner's perspective on these communities. The presence in student texts remains an actual and overt, not only a theorized, fiction of stability. Such writing is by definition problematic, but for more interesting reasons than those that are usually given for its supposedly "lower-level" problems. Within the enclosed discourse of the school, student writing retains its status as practice—no matter how correct, "original," or provocative its text may be. It is always rehearsal, if dress rehearsal, for achieving the privileges of an independent text, and thus it is an emblem for the dependencies of all texts.

3   The Margins of Literacy: "In Education Speaking"

I am not going to close by detailing developments in composition theory or pedagogy that have followed the mandate by Channing and nineteenth-century social circumstances to reconceive writing instruction as instruction for a specifically new student writer. Many new relationships between rhetoric and composition in this century have been explained by others, notably James Berlin in his *Rhetoric and Reality: Writing Instruction in American Colleges, 1900–1985*.[19] Although these developments could contribute to further study of the new student writer and of the particular literacy that is taught in many kinds of contemporary composition instruction, the task that remains here is to place textual rhetoric, composition, and the issue of presence for this new student together in a contemporary version.

The best way to do this is to end where composition always begins, in the writing of students. In particular, we have learned the most about the uncertain yet assertive action that all contemporary writing involves from Mina Shaughnessy's construction of the basic writer, a persona that teachers of composition and a broad range of people in literary studies accepted immediately after the publication of *Errors and Expectations* in 1977.[20] In that characterization, Shaughnessy provided a model for contemporary writing that has allowed us to listen for the first time to the voices of these writers. This voice is heard not as their directly transmitted authoritative speech but as specific missteps that point out exactly how distinct a textual world is and why rhetoric would inevitably be changed to acknowledge its distinctness.

On the surface of Shaughnessy's book, we read her insights about the well-reasoned sources of student errors and her fresh and equally reasoned ways to look for patterns among these errors in student texts. These previously mysterious textual anomalies and her alternatives to older systems for responding to them were immediately taken up and glossed by the work of hundreds of teachers who face similar teaching situations. But the book's subtextual music, especially in its reorchestration of what it means to write, was the force that went to the hearts of its readers, whether or not they had dealt with equally impenetrable student texts.

The heroes of Shaughnessy's book were not teachers, or even Shaughnessy herself, but the students whose writing about the importance of college supplied a counterpoint to customary ideas of what writing is and what this medium means to the writer. One wrote:

> The main point of this topic is that the Children an College students aren't learning to read and write for that they will used later in life. I don't believe society has prepared me for the work I want to do that. is in education speaking, that my main point in being here, If this isn't an essay. of a thousand word's that because I don't have much to say. for it has been four year since I last wrote one, and by the time I am finish here I hope to be able to write a number of essay. (19)

Shaughnessy wrote that she "could only sit there reading and re-reading the alien papers, wondering what had gone wrong and trying to understand" (vii). But she realized, as the book unfolds her progress, that the answer was in this student's text and the others like it. The clues came from very clear phrases: "in education speaking," "my main point in being here," "If this isn't an essay," and "I hope to be able to write." The solution, and the metaphor that makes Shaughnessy's work vital in a broader vision of writing as a discrete medium, was in her word "alien."

Her basic writer became, I would suggest, an active emblem for contemporary writing and for all of its writers' entries into unfamiliar textual worlds. Just as speech and primarily oral situations are always simultaneously confluent with, and alienated from, the fixed product of writing that attempts to record them, every writer is in some measure a basic writer. Shaughnessy's work and that of her followers have outlined and given texture to the specific problematics of writing that is not meant to record, to prepare, to transmit, or to assert an authorized message but to enter tentatively into the textuality that has only recently been created by a modern concatenation of texts.[21]

In many ways, Shaughnessy's work can remind even the most sophisticated students of discourse of their own most basic experiences with the linguistic world that they can now apparently take for granted. Much of what she said estranges us from writing itself, allowing us to defamiliarize this phenomenon and therefore to grasp our need to find a comprehensive theory that accounts for it. By discussing how the tools writers must learn to use and the handwriting they must practice and perfect can interfere with the ideas that a writer is having while composing, Shaughnessy could bring to mind many painful and pleasurable lessons her readers might have forgotten. Depending on one's age, the left-handed reader might recall stupidly humiliating corrections of a young left-handed writer. The book encompassed everyone's investment in handwriting, in learning to type, or in using word processing. Everyone's first personal notebook, favorite pen, and first easy access to cheap paper was recalled. It became clear that the acquisition of unselfconscious writing in our culture was being reenacted in the story of these New York students. Just as primary, textual, and authorial literacies have preceded formalized literary criticism, philosophy of language, and contemporary stylistics, so the basic writer began with scribal writing that developed oral assertiveness and only later might reach textual sophistication.

Shaughnessy's examples systematically point to a strong fit between cultural history and typical individual developments of written discourse. She enumerated the common topics of "thought" and of writing that are in no way commonplace for basic writers and made vivid what writing has demanded from unwritten, nonrhetorical, personal lives. It is impossible to ignore that we are all more at home in "home" rather than in tense and competitive written languages, especially after we enumerate the stances that basic writers must consciously acquire. They appear, for instance, to be "unresponsive" to or to avoid "directly addressing" assignments. They may rely on common wisdom, received opinion, and clichés. They do not state and defend new information in a thesis or place an insight in a prominent place. They retell instead old conclusions and repeat their contexts. They do not stipulate, concede, hierarchically rank, order, discriminate, privilege, or refute, all of the actions that formalized written language involves.

Basic writers remind us, for instance, of the competitive contest that is implied by the advanced act of "marshaling evidence." They assume that such disciplined acts are unnecessary, and that we will believe their points if they tell about a personal experience that reinforces them. The student who wrote "Reality is what I say it is" (238) was in fact speaking for the oral credibility of assertions. This flat generalization, followed by a personal reverie, made it clear that we have many usually hidden and certainly problematic assumptions about how writing actually imitates common thought patterns. Selecting and arranging examples, citing sources, deferring to authority and expertise, acknowledging the case of an opponent, and leaving open the possibility for future correction are not "normal" discourse habits. They are the historical canons of the well-formed text and are opposed to the basic writer's unselfconscious trust that she will be believed. As David Bartholomae, who has extended Shaughnessy's persona of the student as a beginner says in "Inventing the University," all writers, in order to write, must imagine for themselves the privilege of being "insiders" (287). Outside the social milieu around a much older oral rhetoric, no "mere" writer—remedial or not—can escape this demand on imagination.

Conceptual habits are not the only sources of difference between those who might think of writing as a medium for containing and directly communicating clear ideas and those who must acknowledge their embeddedness in textuality. Basic writers' "sentence fragments" are often the result of a normal pattern of thinking, finding a "subject" but once, then following it with many predications in both our thought and our speech. But as fragments of writing, the grammatical fragments produced this way should remind us of our own reverence for the grammatical as well as for the assertive, individual subject who was constructed by much earlier theories. This univocal (speaking) subject turns out to be a product of, not a precedent to, the same impulse toward fixed language and meanings that worried Plato.

That is, the subject in a thought is not a grammatical category, at least not consciously so. The "fragmentation" of discourses has called into question our ideas about one originating fundamental metaphysics, questions that also lead us to imagine the univocal author's "death." This fragmentation takes on yet another cutting edge when it is associated with the sentence fragment itself. This ignorant "illiteracy" is not unintelligent, but it is a clear indicator of the difference between normal thought or speech and writing, wherein making a single statement has been highly valued. Similarly, "missing" verb endings, which are common in the normal speech of many unschooled speakers, do not demonstrate a writer's hopeless stupidity. Rather, they invite us to look carefully at the relation of the individual to overwhelming and inescapable grammars constituting the civilized structures of language that we have made dominant.

Most speakers of English would become anxious if forced to adopt a new language, perhaps one contrived by Borges, whose only word for the color black was "nigger." But adult beginners in writing must equally fragment their loyalties and identities if they are to pass, for the sake of similarly arbitrary and peculiar impositions of the correct. This concept of perfection in language has taken its force from early scribal reproductions of texts. Shakespeare, we remember without malice, spelled his name at least six ways. But he lived in an age developing newly assertive authorship, and used writing only as his tool. He was, we can imagine, relatively unafraid of how it might use him or his speech.

The qualities of basic writing also tell the story of developing discourse *as* discourse. The basic writer's moves from "disorganized" to common, postpicaresque narrative patterns remind us of (and incite some wariness about) the perceived progress of prose forms. A line from Thomas Nashe's curdling Renaissance tales through Smollett's to the formalized achievements of Jane Austen and Thackeray might also trace the slowly learned narrative strategies that all writers must develop. Literary form has become possible by virtue of obvious imitations, as for example in Fielding's parody of Richardson. Formal imitations assert a new genre, or tradition, in which a form may become independent of the story it contains. As studies of these forms add to their tradition by crystallizing a genre's normative power, so does the individual's increasingly schooled writing move from recorded story to imitated pattern to self-conscious, possibly even controlled, unreliable, narration. The typical bed-to-bed patterns in children's early stories ("I got up, I went downstairs . . .") remind us of medieval narratives. Strong plots arrive, in the culture and in thinking about how to tell a story, later.

All of these speculations might be taken to indicate only that basic writers do not know the conventions of written discourse, conventions that ultimately derive from strongly assertive and strongly plotted earlier oral practices. Basic writers, we could infer, have not grasped the dialectic origins of either narrative form or academic exposition. "Crisis" and "climax" are well known to them, but only as personal matters, not as stable locales in fictional worlds or as topics for analysis. Basic writers would speculate, with our own earlier literary biographical forebears, on what Romeo and Juliet's children might have done to settle the family troubles. For them, love and death are real, not "love" and "death."

But we nonetheless cannot say, as the brief student

script quoted earlier and many others demonstrate, that this sort of writing records speech or thought directly. "My main point in being here" is not the innocent, untutored language of the romanticized streets. What happens in basic writing is much more complex. An unwritten, nonrhetorical oral community can be more accurately named. It is the unintended parody of highly literate writing that Ong has called "secondary orality." Basic writers grasp at, but do not yet grasp, overheard, subtextual conventions. As Bartholomae has argued, they show us what they think "sounds right," and thus make us see that "sounding right" must always be in some measure self-conscious, in our own writing as well as in theirs. By not knowing conventions, they show us how arbitrary those conventions are and further demonstrate our desires to elevate the only, the correct, ways to write.

Consequently, their writing leaves us unable to ignore the discourse-as-discourse quality of our own writing and equally unable to reject a theory that tries to acknowledge its multiply voiced and distinct communities. Language speaks through them. They are without our defenses, filters, and conscious processes of selection or, better, of metaselection. Their writing brings up all of the premises I have reviewed and questioned here about independently choosing and shaping or about manipulating the content, form, style, and execution that we equate with rational processes, controlling ideas, and "rhetoric." This writing shows how two-edged "convention" is, how it inevitably contains us before we become free, only provisionally, to use it within a well-marked field of play. Basic writers also, therefore, know conventions better than we do. By virtue of their innocent certainty about being able to learn to write—to directly originate and further to "communicate" in writing—basic writers call into question what we have meant and may mean by authorship.

We, anxiously reading the writing of any student or of any writer whose stance is uncertain, wonder at times if we must not rethink our assumptions and premises about the structures that make a text important. We have assented to the priority of these structures usually without seeing them for the "assumptions" and "premises" they are. By dislocating our comfortably established agendas about what intelligent adults do "naturally" when they write, and about what "intelligent writing" is, basic writers are perhaps the best objective correlatives we could find to inform arguments about the stability and instability, or origins and referents, of writing. In this sense, the strong presence of the basic writer to the texts they leave behind makes us aware of what is at stake in writing. Along with the "historical," "logical," or "empirical" cases this study has considered, basic writing shows that to be a complete and forceful person who "speaks," and to make a point in writing that is "clear" to all, is a problematic identity that requires us to fictionalize, not to re-create, stable meanings.

The basic writer's common suspicion of English teachers, like our own repressed worries about measuring up, is an emblem for suspicions about being appropriated into any unfamiliar system. This caution also symbolizes the pain of these inevitable appropriations. All who become writers—and, later, become "written" or textual figures—experience it. But a beginner's determination to learn to write also comments on this cautious response to writing because the beginner knows, however unspecifically, that writing well is an invitation to belong to more than one world. Basic writers are therefore willing *bricoleurs*. They write as if—despite, and in the face of, writing itself. As Shaughnessy wrote, alone in her study, and as I have attempted to specify here, "writing is . . . an expanding world of competencies that interact and collide and finally merge" (287).

Notes

Bibliography

Index

Notes

Introduction

1. The position I take differs from Knoblauch and Brannon's objections to classical rhetoric's applications in writing instruction. Their study (Upper Montclair, NJ: Boyton/Cook, 1984) and mine share many goals, but mine asserts that "epistemic" rhetoric was always theorized, and that intertextuality was made possible by actual discursive practices in written forms, not by new modes of "thought." Historically changing answers to "what does it mean to write?" separate oral rhetoric from the textual rhetoric that will be proposed here.

2. *Journal of Basic Writing* 5.1 (1986): 4–23. Bartholomae states this position and makes references to supporting work, notably Patricia Bizzell, "College Composition: Initiation into the Academic Discourse Communities," *Curriculum Inquiry* 12 (1982): 191–207.

1 Contemporary Configurations of Writing: Textual Rhetoric

1. In Jane P. Tompkins, "The Reader in History," *Reader-Response Criticism*, ed. Jane Tompkins (Baltimore: Johns Hopkins UP, 1980) 201–32.

2. See Roland Barthes, "To Write: An Intransitive Verb?" *S/Z*, trans. Richard Howard (New York: Hill and Wang, 1986) 19.

3. (Chicago: U of Chicago P, 1983) 47.

4. *Language, Counter-Memory, Practice*, ed. Donald F. Bouchard, trans. Donald Bouchard and Sherry Simon (Ithaca, NY: Cornell UP, 1977) 115.

5. *Orality and Literacy* (London: Methuen, 1982) 175–79. See also his "The Writer's Audience Is Always a Fiction," *PMLA* 90 (1975): 9–22.

6. See Lloyd Bitzer, "The Rhetorical Situation," *Contemporary*

Theories of Rhetoric: Selected Readings, ed. Richard L. Johaneson (New York: Harper, 1971) 381–94.

7. Carole Blair, "Nietzsche's Lecture Notes on Rhetoric: A Translation," *Philosophy and Rhetoric* 16.2 (1983): 96–98.

8. *The Pedagogical Imperative: Teaching as A Literary Genre*, Yale French Studies 63, ed. Barbara Johnson (New Haven: Yale UP, 1982) 19.

9. Frederick Nietzsche, *Gesammelte Werke* (Munich: Musarion Verlag, 1922) 5: 300; cited by Paul deMan, *Allegories of Reading: Figural Language in Rousseau, Nietzsche, Rilke, and Proust* (New Haven: Yale UP, 1979) 105–6.

10. *English Literature in the Sixteenth Century* (Oxford: Clarendon, 1954) 61.

11. See Jonathan Culler, *The Pursuit of Signs: Semiotics, Literature, Deconstruction* (Ithaca, NY: Cornell UP, 1981).

12. (New York: Harcourt, 1956) 24.

13. See "The Resistance to Theory," *The Pedagogical Imperative: Teaching as a Literary Genre* 3–20.

14. Susan Suleiman, introduction, *The Reader in the Text*, ed. Susan Suleiman and Inge Crosman (Princeton: Princeton UP, 1980) 13–14.

15. Lloyd Bitzer, introduction, *The Philosophy of Rhetoric*, by George Campbell (Carbondale: Southern Illinois UP, 1963) ix–xxxvii.

16. Trans. Richard Miller (New York: Hill and Wang, 1974) 174.

17. *Inventions: Writing, Textuality, and Understanding in Literary History* (New Haven: Yale UP, 1982) 71–2.

18. (Chicago: U of Chicago P, 1983) 49.

19. See e.g., Gérard Genette, "Rhétorique et Enseignement," *Figures II* (Paris: Éditions du Sevil, 1969) 23–42, for a description of how the study of literature continued naturally from rhetorical instruction in the art of composition. He shows how nineteenth-century rhetorical instructional terms became twentieth-century critical categories.

20. What follows is most heavily (if ironically) indebted to Dell Hymes, "The Ethnography of Speaking," *Readings in the Sociology of Language*, ed. Joshua A. Fishman (The Hague: Moulton, 1968) 99–138. It also draws from James Kinneavy, "The Relation of the Whole to the Parts in Interpretation Theory and in the Composing Process," *Linguistics, Stylistics, and the Teaching of Composition* (Akron, OH: Akron U Dept. of English, 1979) 1–23; and Lloyd Bitzer, "The Rhetorical Situation."

21. See Joseph M. Williams, "The English Language as a Use-

Governed Behavior," *Style and Variables in English,* ed. Timothy Shopen and Joseph M. Williams (Cambridge, MA: Winthrop, 1981) 44.

22. "Textual context" encompasses both "history," or precedents, and "intertextuality," which is "not the investigation of sources and influences as traditionally conceived; it casts its net wider to include anonymous discursive practices, codes whose origins are lost, that make possible the signifying practices of later texts" (Culler 103).

23. *Saving the Text: Literature, Derrida, Philosophy* (Baltimore: Johns Hopkins UP, 1981) xxi.

24. See, e.g., Jack Goody, "The Grand Dichotomy Reconsidered," *The Domestication of the Savage Mind* (Cambridge: Cambridge UP, 1977) 163–67; Walter Ong, "Rhetoric and Consciousness," *Rhetoric, Romance, and Technology* 2 and passim. I am also questioning, at least on this point, Eric Havelock's definition of writing: "All systems which use scratching or drawing or painting to think with or feel with are irrelevant. . . . A successful or developed writing system . . . does not think at all. It should be the purely passive instrument of the spoken word." (*Origins of Western Literacy,* Monograph Series 14 [N.p.: Ontario Institute for Studies in Education, n.d.] 17).

25. See, e.g., Barry M. Kroll and Roberta J. Vann, eds., *Exploring Speaking-Writing Relations: Connections and Contrasts* (Urbana, IL: NCTE, 1981).

26. See "From Utterance to Text: The Bias of Language in Speech and Writing," *Harvard Educational Review* 47.3 (August 1977): 257–81, and "On Language and Literacy," *International Journal of Psycholinguistics* 7.1–2 [17/18] (1980): 69–83.

27. Jacques Derrida, *Spurs: Nietzsche's Styles,* trans. Barbara Harlow (Chicago: U of Chicago P, 1978).

28. I am indebted to Joseph Williams for pointing out this figure and its implications in hierarchical explanations of texts and their generation.

2 Historical Configurations of Writing: The Space before the Reader

1. Quoted by Felix Reichmann, *The Sources of Western Literacy: The Middle Eastern Civilizations* (Westport, CT: Greenwood, 1980) 88–89.

2. See Moses Hadas, *Ancilla to Classical Reading* (New York: Columbia UP, 1961) 12–13.

3. Frederic G. Kenyon, *Books and Readers in Ancient Greece and Rome,* 2nd ed. (Oxford: Clarendon, 1951) 19–20.

4. James Bowen, *A History of Western Education*, vol. 1 (New York: St. Martin's, 1972) 71–2.

5. E.g., Ong, *Orality and Literacy*; Barry M. Kroll and Roberta J. Vann, eds., *Exploring Speaking-Writing Relationships: Connections and Contrasts*; Jack Goody, *The Domestication of the Savage Mind*; Jack Goody, ed., *Literacy in Traditional Societies* (Cambridge: Cambridge UP, 1968); David Olson, "From Utterance to Text: The Bias of Language in Speech and Writing"; "Literacy and the Future of Print," ed. George Gerbner, *Journal of Communication* 30 (1980): 89–205.

6. See Frances Yates, *The Art of Memory* (Harmondsworth: Penguin, 1969) 42–62.

7. See Werner Jaeger, "The Rhetoric of Isocrates and Its Cultural Ideal," *The Province of Rhetoric*, eds. Joseph Schwartz and John A. Rycinga (New York: Ronald, 1965) 84–111.

8. Trans. George Norlin, 3 vols. (Cambridge, MA: Harvard UP; London: Heinemann, 1928). Citations are from this edition.

9. Quoted by Edward S. Forster, ed., *Isocrates: Cyprian Orations* (New York: Arno, 1979) 23.

10. *The Province of Rhetoric* 125.

11. Ed. with an introduction by Stephen G. Nichols, Jr. (New Haven: Yale UP, 1963) 25.

12. The standard treatment of this early education is H. I. Marrou, *A History of Education in Antiquity*, trans. George Lamb (New York: Sheed and Ward, 1956); see also George Kennedy, *The Art of Persuasion in Greece* (Princeton: Princeton UP, 1963) and *The Art of Rhetoric in the Roman World* (Princeton: Princeton UP, 1972).

13. See Richard Sennet, *The Fall of Public Man* (New York: Knopf, 1977). We are, of course, only recently encouraging the rise of public woman; see Walter Ong, *Fighting for Life: Contest, Sexuality, and Consciousness* (Ithaca, NY: Cornell UP, 1981), for an account of sexuality and education.

14. See, e.g., Adams Sherman Hill (Boylston Professor of Rhetoric and Oratory, Harvard University), *Our English* (New York: Chautauqua, 1890) 12–15.

15. [Cicero] *I*, trans. H. Caplin, ed. G. P. Goold, 2 vols. (London: Loeb, 1981) 1:32–33. The citations are to the Loeb edition.

16. *Institutes*, trans. H. E. Butler, ed. G. P. Goold, 4 vols. (London : Loeb, 1980) 3:2; bk.10. The citations are to the Loeb edition, followed by the book number.

17. M. T. Clanchy, *From Memory to Written Record: England, 1066–1307* (London: Arnold, 1979) 218. For a treatment of specific historical relations between writing tools and changing composing processes, see Elizabeth Larsen, "A History of the Composing Process," diss., U of Wisconsin-Milwaukee, 1983.

18. Clanchy ibid. See also 195–97.

19. Clanchy 181.

20. Clanchy 216–17. See also 88, 97, 181, 183, 227.

21. Quoted by John Burrow, "The Medieval Compendium," *Times Literary Supplement*, 21 May 1976, 615.

22. See Tertullian, *Tertullian against Praxeas*, trans. A. Souter (London: n.p., 1920) 36–37, par. 5, for a third-century explanation of *Logos*: "Whatsoever you think is word; whatsoever you understand is speech."

23. Augustine, *Confessions*, trans. Vernon J. Bourke, *Writings of Saint Augustine*, vol. 13, *Fathers of the Church*, 33 vols. (Washington, DC: Catholic U of America P, 1953) 20, 21.

24. Clanchy 90, with quotations from the Oxford UP ed. (1969–) of Orderic Vitalis, *Historia Ecclesiastica*, ed. Majorie Chibnall 2:360–61; bk. 4.

25. (Cleveland: Meridian, 1957) 33–34.

26. *The Implications of Literacy: Written Language and Models of Interpretation in the Eleventh and Twelfth Centuries* (Princeton: Princeton UP, 1983) 272–81.

27. Pp. 241–57; see pl. 5.

28. See Culler, *On Deconstruction*, (Ithaca, NY: Cornell UP, 1982) 125, and Jacques Derrida, *Margins of Philosophy*, trans. Alan Bass (Chicago: U of Chicago P, 1982) 330.

29. *The Principles of Letter-Writing* (1137), *Three Medieval Rhetorical Arts*, trans. and ed. James J. Murphy (Berkeley: U of California P, 1971) 10.

30. *New Poetics* (1208–13), *Three Arts*, trans. James Baltyell Kopp, ed. Murphy 34.

31. *Orality and Literacy* 11.

32. See Alvin Kernan, *Printing Technology, Letters and Samuel Johnson* (Princeton: Princeton UP, 1987) 11 and passim.

33. *The Civilization of the Renaissance in Italy*, trans. S. G. C. Middlemore, 2nd ed. (Oxford: Oxford UP, 1945) 81.

34. 2 vols. (Cambridge: Cambridge UP, 1979) 1:228, n.

35. See, e.g., James Murphy, *Rhetoric in the Middle Ages* 357–74.

36. Burkhardt 81.

37. *Literary Language and Its Public in Late Latin Antiquity and in the Middle Ages*, trans. Ralph Manheim, Bollingen Series 74 (New York: Pantheon, 1965) 254.

38. See G. Gregory Smith, *Elizabethan Critical Essays* 2 vols. (Oxford UP, 1946) 2:5.

39. Smith 1:308.

40. Smith 2:366–67. Further citations from Smith are in the text.

41. G. B. Harrison, ed., *Elizabethan and Jacobean Quartos* (New York: Barnes, 1966) 80.

42. See Peter Stallybrass and Allon White, *The Politics and Poetics of Transgression* (Ithaca, NY: Cornell UP, 1986) 27–79, for a thorough investigation of Jonson's contributions to new Renaissance authorship.

43. Auerbach 242.

44. Eisenstein 229.

45. See Ben Jonson, *Discoveries: A Critical Edition with an Introduction and Notes on the True Purport and Genesis of the Book*, ed. Maurice Castelain (Paris: Librairie Hachette and Cie, 1906) passim. For a summary of the relation of rhetorical education and the development of classical imitation in the Renaissance, see Walter Ong, "Tudor Writings on Rhetoric," *Studies in the Renaissance* 15 (1968): 39–69; see also Joel B. Altman, *The Tudor Play of Mind: Rhetorical Inquiry and the Development of Elizabethan Drama* (Berkeley: U of California P, 1978) esp. 43–53.

46. Quoted in William Harrison Woodward, *Studies in Education during the Age of the Renaissance, 1400–1600* (New York: Russell and Russell, 1965) 200.

47. *Timber*, ed. Harrison 22.

48. David Cressy, *Literacy and the Social Order: Reading and Writing in Tudor and Stuart England* (Cambridge: Cambridge UP, 1980) 76–77.

49. Quoted by Cressy 4.

50. Edwin Johnston Howard, ed. (1533; rpt. Oxford, OH: Anchor, 1946) 5–7.

51. Quoted by Richard Foster Jones, *The Triumph of the English Language: A Survey of Opinions Concerning the Vernacular from the Introduction of Printing to the Restoration* (Stanford: Stanford UP, 1953) 29–30.

52. (Chicago: U of Chicago P, 1977) 85–89 and passim.

53. See Joseph Williams, *Style: Ten Lessons in Clarity and Grace* (Glenview, IL: Scott, Foresman, 1981) 7–14.

54. Edmund Coote, *The English Schoole-Maister* (1596; rpt. Menston, England: Scolar, 1968) 32. See Cressy 21, and Michael Stubbs, *Language and Literacy* (London: Routledge and Kegan Paul, 1980) 43–69, esp. 44–49 and 68–69.

55. Rpt. ed. (Menston, England: Scolar, 1971).

56. Ed. with introduction and notes by Forrest G. Robinson (Indianapolis: Bobbs, 1970) 30. All quotations are from this edition.

57. See John Guillory, *Poetic Authority: Spenser, Milton and Literary History* (New York: Columbia UP, 1983) for an interpretation

of this phenomena on the grounds of a shift from "sacred" to "secular" authority and from "inspiration" to "imagination."

58. (Cambridge, MA: Harvard UP, 1971) 61–65.

59. See works cited by Hirsch and Williams; Richard Lanham, *Revising Prose* (New York: Scribner's, 1979); Robert de Beaugrande, *Text, Discourse, and Process: Toward a Multidisciplinary Science of Texts* (Norwood, NJ: Ablex, 1980).

60. *Some Notes toward a Theory of Allegorical Rhetoric in the English Renaissance* (Chicago: U of Chicago P, 1969) 172; *Timber*, ed. Harrison 95.

61. See George Kennedy, *Greek Rhetoric under Christian Emperors* (Princeton: Princeton UP, 1983) 119, 141, 145.

62. See, e.g., Stanley Fish, *Self-Consuming Artifacts* (Berkeley: U of California P, 1972); Joan Webber, *The Eloquent "I"* (Madison: U of Wisconsin P, 1968); Stephen Greenblatt, *Renaissance Self-Fashioning* (Chicago: U of Chicago P, 1980).

3   Philosophy Confronts Writing:
Plato's *Gorgias* and *Phaedrus*

1. (Chapel Hill: U of North Carolina P) 19.

2. See Havelock, *Preface to Plato* (Cambridge, MA: Belknap Press of Harvard UP, 1963) 19.

3. Havelock's closely reasoned explanation of Plato's rejection of poetry views Plato as rejecting oral, heroic individualism in favor of literate self-consciousness and distancing. See also Robert Connors, "Greek Rhetoric and the Transition from Orality," *Philosophy and Rhetoric* 19.1 (1986): 38–65, who has made a similar suggestion about the relation between epic recitation and oratorical performances.

4. Walter Hamilton, trans., introduction, *Gorgias*, by Plato (Harmondsworth: Penguin, 1960) 7–18. Citations are to this text, chosen for its wide availability.

5. See Virginia N. Steinhoff, "The *Phaedrus* Idyll as Ethical Play: The Platonic Stance," *The Rhetorical Tradition and Modern Writing*, ed. James Murphy (New York: MLA, 1982) 31–45.

6. Stanley Fish, "The Aesthetics of the Good Physician," *Self-Consuming Artifacts* 1–77; Jacques Derrida, "Plato's Pharmacy," *Disseminations*, trans. Barbara Johnson (Chicago: U of Chicago P, 1981) 61–172. Two other rhetorical readings of the dialogue are relevant: Richard Weaver, "The *Phaedrus* and the Nature of Rhetoric," *The Ethics of Rhetoric* (Chicago: Henry Regnery, 1953) 3–26, and Ronna Burger, *Plato's Phaedrus: A Defense of the Philosophical Art of Writing* (Tuscaloosa: U of Alabama P, 1980).

7. Plato, *Phaedrus*, trans. with introduction by W. C. Helmbold and W. G. Rabinowitz (Indianapolis: Bobbs, 1956) 228. This edition is cited because it is widely available.

8. Burger, "The Art of Writing" 90–114.

9. This paradox and its development control Derrida's reading.

4   Writing Confronts Rhetoric: Changing Definitions

1. *On Christian Doctrine: The Enchiridion*, trans. J. F. Shaw (Edinburgh: T and T Clark, 1873) 121. Further citations will be to this edition.

2. "Autobiography and Narrative," *Reconstructing Individualism: Autonomy, Individuality, and the Self in Western Thought*, ed. Thomas C. Heller, Morton Sosma, and David Wellbery (Stanford, CA: Stanford UP, 1986) 16.

3. Desiderius Erasmus, *On Copia of Words and Ideas*, trans. Donald B. King and H. David Rix (Milwaukee, WI: Marquette UP, 1963) 86.

4. *The Cornucopian Text: Problems of Writing in the French Renaissance* (Oxford: Clarendon, 1979) xi. Cave's analysis of writing in the French Renaissance supports the view of English developments that are treated here and below.

5. Ramus has been transmitted largely through the works of Walter Ong: e.g., *Ramus, Method, and the Decay of Dialogue* (Cambridge, MA: Harvard UP, 1958), and "Ramist Method and the Commercial Mind," *Rhetoric, Romance and Technology* (Ithaca: Cornell UP, 1971) 165–89. See also Wilbur Samuel Howell, *Logic and Rhetoric in England, 1500–1700* (New York: Russell and Russell, 1961) 146–281 and passim.

6. *The Advancement of Learning*, ed. James Spedding, Robert Leslie Ellis, and Douglas Denon Heath, new ed., vol. 3 of *The Works of Francis Bacon*, 7 vols. (London: Longmans, et. al., 1876) 283.

7. See Richard Altick, *The English Common Reader* (Chicago: U of Chicago P, 1957).

8. This possibility is the subject of Alvin Kernan's *Printing Technology, Letters, and Samuel Johnson*.

9. Ed. Douglas Ehringer (Carbondale: Southern Illinois UP, 1963).

10. 2nd ed. (London: Longmans, 1869) v.

11. *Eighteenth-Century British Logic and Rhetoric* (Princeton: Princeton UP, 1971) 153.

12. Thomas Sheridan, *A Course of Lectures on Elocution: Together with Two Dissertations on Language* (London: Strahan, 1762; reissued New York: Blom, 1968) 163.

13. (London: Oxford UP, 1936) 3.

14. *A Rhetoric of Motives* (Berkeley: U of California P, 1969) 22.

15. *The Philosophy of Literary Form*, 3rd ed. (Berkeley: U of California P, 1973) 216.

16. *A Rhetoric of Motives* 62.

17. Trans. John Wilkinson and Purcell Weaver (Notre Dame: U of Notre Dame P, 1969) 5.

18. *Human Understanding*, vol. 1 (Princeton: Princeton UP, 1972) 264.

19. *Roots for a New Rhetoric* (New York: Russell and Russell, 1959) 57.

5   The Educational Result: Rhetoric and Composition

1. See, e.g., William Riley Parker, "Where Do English Departments Come From?" *College English* 28 (1967): 339–51; Albert R. Kitzhaber, "Rhetoric in American Colleges, 1850–1890," diss., U of Washington, 1953; Richard Braddock, Richard Lloyd-Jones, and Lowell Schoer, *Research in Written Composition* (Urbana, IL: NCTE, 1963).

2. See Lee A. Sonnino, "Some Theoretical Implications of Rhetorical Practice," *A Handbook to Sixteenth-Century Rhetoric* (London: Routledge and Kegan Paul, 1968) 10–14.

3. Richard Whately, as noted earlier, explicitly addresses writing in the traditional historical study of transmitted rhetoric. After he asserts the importance of writing, however, his *Elements of Rhetoric* (1826) returns to argumentation without further references to composing in writing. See above, chap. 4.

4. Francois Furet and Jacques Ozouf, Cambridge Studies in Oral and Literate Culture (Cambridge: Cambridge UP, 1982) 74. See *The English Common Reader* esp. 141–87.

5. *Classical Rhetoric for the Modern Student* 594–630. Cf. Susan Miller, " 'Is There a Text in This Class?' " *Freshman English News* 11 (1982): 23, and Patrick Scott, "Jonathan Maxcy and the Aims of Early Nineteenth-Century Rhetorical Teaching," *College English* 45 (1983): 21–22.

6. See George Kennedy, *Greek Rhetoric under Christian Emperors* (Princeton: Princeton UP, 1983), on *Koinē* Greek and a complete rhetoric education based on style: 46–7, 119.

7. Sonnino, *Handbook* 4–6.

8. Warren Guthrie, "The Development of Rhetorical Theory in America, 1," *Speech Monographs* 13 (1946): 14–18.

9. See S. Michael Halloran, "Rhetoric in the American College Curriculum: The Decline of Public Discourse," *Pre/Text* 3 (1982): 260.

10. See Warren Guthrie, "The Development of Rhetorical Theory in America: 1635–1850," pt. 4, *Speech Monographs* 16 (1949): 99, who cites John Witherspoon's treatment of the ends of discourse, from *Lectures on Moral Philosophy and Eloquence* (1810).

11. See Ronald F. Reid, "The Boylston Professorship of Rhetoric and Oratory, 1806–1904: A Case Study of Changing Concepts of Rhetoric and Pedagogy," *Quarterly Journal of Speech* 45 (1959): 239–57; Dorothy I. Anderson and Waldo W. Braden, eds., *Ellery T. Channing, Lectures Read to the Seniors at Harvard College* (Carbondale: Southern Illinois UP, 1968) xiii–xx; and Wallace Douglas, "Rhetoric for the Meritocracy," *English in America*, ed. Richard Ohmann (New York: Oxford UP, 1976) 100–13.

12. Douglas 103.

13. *Ellery T. Channing* 15. Citations are from this text.

14. See Richard Young, "Paradigms and Problems: Needed Research in Rhetorical Invention," *Research on Composing*, ed., Lee Odell and Charles R. Cooper (Urbana, IL: NCTE, 1978) 29–48, for a summary opposition to what Young sees as the negative influence of romantic "vitalism" on fostering the faculties.

15. Halloran 254.

16. *Ellery T. Channing* xxix, x–vii.

17. *Ellery T. Channing* 194–96. For curricular developments reinforcing this aspect of Channing's thought, see Arthur H. Applebee, *Tradition and Reform in the Teaching of English: A History* (Urbana, IL: NCTE, 1974); Stephen Tchudi, "Composition and Rhetoric in American Secondary Schools 1840–1900," *English Journal* 68 (1979): 34–39; Gene L. Piché, "Class and Culture in the Development of the High School English Curriculum," *Research in the Teaching of English* 11 (1977): 17–27; Albert Kitzhaber, "Rhetoric in American Colleges 1850–1900."

18. See Walter Ong, "Residual Orality in Academia," *Fighting for Life: Contest, Sexuality, and Consciousness* (Ithaca: Cornell UP, 1981) 125–29.

19. Carbondale: Southern Illinois UP, 1987.

20. New York: Oxford UP, 1977.

21. See esp. Andrea Lunsford, "The Content of Basic Writers' Essays," *CCC* 31 (1980): 278–90, and all issues of the *Journal of Basic Writing*.

Bibliography

This bibliography includes the works cited in the notes and other references that have been important resources. The items in this list are grouped according to five usually separate ways of thinking and talking about the issues that I have joined in this study. History of instruction in composition and its theories, technological and theoretical studies of literacy, works about literary composition in many historical settings, literary theory and criticism, and history and theory of rhetoric are the established categories of interest I have relied on to address problems of rhetoric and writing.

Many contemporary theorists propose that ideas emerge from struggles among ostensibly separate discourses, not from within them. This has certainly been the case in this attempt to see how resources in each of these categories comment on analogues and contrary views in the others.

Composition: History of Instruction and Theory

Allen, P. David, and Dorothy J. Watson. *Findings of Research in Miscue Analysis*. Urbana, IL: NCTE, 1976.

Applebee, Arthur N. *Tradition and Reform in the Teaching of English: A History*. Urbana, IL: NCTE, 1974.

Baldwin, Charles Sears. *Composition: Oral and Written*. New York: Longmans, 1918.

Bartholomae, David. "Inventing the University." *Journal of Basic Writing* 5.1 (1986): 4–23.

———. "The Study of Error." *CCC* 31 (1980): 253–69.

Bazerman, Charles. "What Written Knowledge Does: Three Examples of Academic Discourse." *Philosophy of the Social Sciences* 2 (September 1981): 361–89.

Bernstein, Basil. *Class, Codes, and Control: Theoretic Studies Toward a Sociology of Language*. London: Routledge and Kegan Paul, 1971.

Braddock, Richard, Richard Lloyd-Jones, and Lowell Schoer. *Research in Written Composition*. Urbana, IL: NCTE, 1963.

Coles, William E. *Composing: Writing as a Self-Creating Process.* Rochelle Park, NJ: Hayden, 1974.

Connors, Robert J. "The Rise and Fall of the Modes of Discourse." *CCC* 32 (1981): 444–63.

Coote, Edmund. *The English Schoole-Maister.* 1596. Menston, England: Scolar, 1968.

Corbett, Edward P. J. *Classical Rhetoric for the Modern Student.* 2nd ed. New York: Oxford UP, 1971.

D'Angelo, Frank. *A Conceptual Theory of Rhetoric.* Cambridge, MA: Winthrop, 1975.

De Beaugrande, Robert. *Text, Discourse, and Process: Toward a Multidisciplinary Science of Texts.* Norwood, NJ: Ablex, 1980.

Douglas, Wallace. "Rhetoric for the Meritocracy." *English in America.* Ed. Richard Ohmann. New York: Oxford UP, 1976. 97–132.

Elyot, Thomas. *Of The Knowledge Which Maketh a Wise Man.* Ed. Edwin Johnston Howard. 1553. Oxford, OH: Anchor, 1946.

Faigley, Lester. "Competing Theories of Process: A Critique and a Proposal." *CE* 48 (1986): 527–42.

Frye, Northrop. "Elementary Teaching and Elementary Scholarship." *PMLA* 79 (1964): 11–18.

Graves, Donald. "An Examination of the Writing Processes of Seven-Year-Old Children." *RTE* 9 (1975): 227–41.

Great Britain. Department of Education and Science. *A Language for Life.* The Bullock Report. London: HMSO, 1975.

Heath, Shirley Brice. "The Development of American Writing Instruction." *Writing: The Nature, Development and Teaching of Written Communication.* Ed. Marcia Farr Whiteman. Hillsdale, NJ: Erlbaum, 1981. 32–38.

Hill, Adams Sherman. *Our English.* New York: Chautauqua, 1890.

Hirsch, E. D. *The Philosophy of Composition.* Chicago: U of Chicago P, 1977.

Horner, Winifred. "Speech-act and Text-act Theory: Themeing in Freshman Composition." *CCC* 30 (1979): 166–69.

Hunt, Kellog. *Grammatical Structures Written at Three Grade Levels.* Urbana, IL: NCTE, 1965.

Hymes, Dell. "The Ethnography of Speaking." *Readings in the Sociology of Language.* Ed. Joshua A. Fishman. The Hague: Moulton, 1968. 99–138.

Johnson, Ralph. *The Scholar's Guide.* 1665. Menston, England: Scolar, 1971.

Kinneavy, James. "The Relation of the Whole to the Parts in Interpretation Theory and in the Composing Process." *Linguistics, Stylistics, and the Teaching of Composition.* Ed. Donald Mc-

Quade. Akron, OH: U of Akron Depart. of English, 1979. 1–
23.

———. *A Theory of Discourse: The Aims of Discourse*. Englewood Cliffs,
NJ: Prentice-Hall, 1971.

Kitzhaber, Albert. "Rhetoric in American Colleges 1850–1900." Diss.
U of Washington, 1953.

———. *Themes, Theories, and Therapy*. New York: McGraw-Hill, 1963.

Knoblauch, Cy, and Lillian Brannon. *Rhetorical Traditions and the
Teaching of Writing*. Upper Montclair, NJ: Boyton/Cook,
1984.

Krashen, Stephen. *Second Language Acquisition and Second Language
Learning*. New York: Pergamon, 1981.

Kroll, Barry M., and John Schafer. "Error-Analysis and the Teaching
of Composition." CCC 29 (1978): 242–48.

Kroll, Barry, and Roberta J. Vann, eds. *Exploring Speaking-Writing
Relationships: Connections and Contrasts*. Urbana, IL: NCTE,
1981.

Lanham, Richard. *Revising Prose*. New York: Scribner's, 1979.

Larsen, Elizabeth. "A History of the Composing Process." Diss. U of
Wisconsin-Milwaukee, 1983.

Lunsford, Andrea. "The Content of Basic Writers' Essays." CCC 31
(1980): 278–90.

Maimon, Elaine P., Gerald L. Belcher, Gail W. Hearn, Barbara F.
Nodine, and Finbarr W. O'Connor. *Writing in the Arts and
Sciences*. Boston: Little, 1981.

Marrou, H. I. *A History of Education in Antiquity*. Trans. George Lamb.
New York: Sheed and Ward, 1956.

Miller, Susan. "'Is There a Text in This Class?' " *Freshman English
News* 11 (1982): 20–24.

———. "What Does it Mean to Be Able to Write?: The Question of
Writing in the Disciplines of Literature and Composition."
College English 45 (1983): 219–35.

Moffett, James. *Teaching the Universe of Discourse*. Boston: Houghton,
1968.

Moran, Michael G., and Ronald F. Lunsford, eds. *Research in Composition and Rhetoric: A Bibliographic Sourcebook*. Westport, CT:
Greenwood, 1984.

North, Stephen M. *The Making of Knowledge in Composition: Portrait
of an Emerging Field*. Upper Montclair, NJ: Boynton/Cook,
1987.

Olson, David. "From Utterance to Text: The Bias of Language in
Speech and Writing." *Harvard Educational Review* 47.3 (August
1977): 257–81.

————. "On Language and Literacy." *International Journal of Psycholin-guistics* 7–1/2 [17/18] (1980): 69–83.

Ong, Walter. *Fighting for Life: Contest, Sexuality, and Consciousness.* Ithaca, NY: Cornell UP, 1981.

Parker, William Riley. "Where Do English Departments Come From?" *College English* 28 (1967): 339–51.

Perl, Sondra. "The Composing Processes of Unskilled College Writers." *RTE* 13 (1979): 317–36.

Piché, Gene L. "Class and Culture in the Development of the High School English Curriculum." *Research in the Teaching of English* 11 (1977): 17–27.

Pike, Kenneth, Alton Becker, and Richard Young. *Rhetoric: Discovery and Change.* New York: Harcourt, 1970.

Scott, Patrick. "Jonathan Maxcy and the Aims of Early Nineteenth-Century Rhetorical Teaching." *College English* 45 (1983): 21–30.

Shaughnessy, Mina. *Errors and Expectations: A Guide for the Teacher of Basic Writing.* New York: Oxford UP, 1977.

Shayer, David. *The Teaching of English in Schools, 1900–1970.* London: Routledge and Kegan Paul, 1972.

Tate, Gary, ed. *Teaching Composition: Ten Bibliographic Essays.* Forth Worth: Texas Christian UP, 1976.

Tchudi, Stephen. "Composition and Rhetoric in American Secondary Schools, 1840–1900." *English Journal* 68 (1979): 34–39.

Thach, C. C. "The Essentials of English Composition to be Taught in Secondary Schools." *Journal of Proceedings and Addresses, National Education Association of the United States.* 37th Annual Meeting. Washington, DC: NCTE, 1898.

Williams, Joseph. "The English Language as Use-Governed Behavior." *Style and Variables in English.* Eds. Timothy Shopen and Joseph M. Williams. Cambridge, MA: Winthrop, 1981. 27–60.

————. "The Phenomenology of Error." *CCC* 32 (1981): 152–68.

————. *Style: Ten Lessons in Clarity and Grace.* Glenview, IL: Scott, 1981.

Winterowd, W. Ross. "Black Holes, Indeterminacy, and Paulo Fiere." *Rhetoric Review* 2 (1983): 28–35.

Woodward, William Harrison. *Studies in Education during the Age of the Renaissance 1400–1600.* New York: Russell and Russell, 1965.

Young, Richard. "Paradigms and Problems: Needed Research in Rhetorical Invention." *Research on Composing.* Ed. Lee Odell and Charles R. Cooper. Urbana, IL: NCTE, 1978. 29–48.

Literacy: Theories and Technological History

Altick, Richard. *The English Common Reader: A Social History of the Mass Reading Public, 1800–1900*. Chicago: U of Chicago P, 1957.

Bowen, James. *A History of Western Education*. 3 vols. New York: St. Martin's, 1972–81. Vol. 1.

Burrow, John. "The Medieval Compendium." *Times Literary Supplement*. 21 May 1976: 615.

Cave, Terrance C. *The Cornucopian Text: Problems of Writing in the French Renaissance*. Oxford: Clarendon, 1979.

Clanchy, M. T. *From Memory to Written Record: England, 1066–1307*. London: Arnold, 1979.

Cressy, David. *Literacy and the Social Order: Reading and Writing in Tudor and Stuart England*. Cambridge: Cambridge UP, 1980.

Eisenstein, Elizabeth. *The Printing Press as an Agent of Change*. 2 vols. Cambridge: Cambridge UP, 1979.

Foucault, Michel. *Discipline and Punish: The Birth of the Prison*. Trans. Alan Sheridan. New York: Vintage, 1979.

Furet, Francois, and Jacques Ozouf. *Reading and Writing: Literacy in France from Calvin to Jules Ferry*. Cambridge Studies in Oral and Literate Culture. Cambridge: Cambridge UP, 1982.

Gerbner, George, ed. "Literacy and the Future of Print." *Journal of Communication* 30 (1980): 89–205.

Goody, Jack, ed. *The Domestication of the Savage Mind*. Cambridge: Cambridge UP, 1977.

———. *Literacy in Traditional Societies*. Cambridge: Cambridge UP, 1968.

Hadas, Moses. *Ancilla to Classical Reading*. New York: Columbia UP, 1961.

Havelock, Eric. *The Literate Revolution in Greece and Its Cultural Consequences*. Princeton: Princeton UP, 1982.

———. *Origins of Western Literacy*. Monograph Series 14. N.p.: Ontario Institute for Studies in Education, n.d.

Jones, Richard Foster. *The Triumph of the English Language: A Survey of Opinions Concerning the Vernacular from the Introduction of Printing to the Restoration*. Stanford: Stanford UP, 1953.

Kenyon, Frederic G. *Books and Readers in Ancient Greece and Rome*. 2nd ed. Oxford: Clarendon, 1951.

McLuhan, Marshall. *The Gutenberg Galaxy: The Making of Typographic Man*. Toronto: U of Toronto P, 1962.

———. *Understanding Media: The Extensions of Man*. New York: McGraw-Hill, 1965.

Olson, David. "From Utterance to Text: the Bias of Language in Speech and Writing." *Harvard Educational Review* 47.3 (August 1977): 257–81.

Ong, Walter. *Interfaces of the Word: Studies in the Evolution of Consciousness and Culture.* Ithaca, NY: Cornell UP, 1977.

———. *Orality and Literacy: The Technologizing of the Word.* London: Methuen, 1982.

———. *Rhetoric, Romance, and Technology.* Ithaca and London: Cornell UP, 1971.

Panofsky, Erwin. *Gothic Architecture and Scholasticism.* Cleveland: Meridian, 1957.

Pattison, Robert. *On Literacy: The Politics of the Word from Homer to the Age of Rock.* New York: Oxford UP, 1982.

Price, Derek Solar. *Science Since Babylon.* New Haven: Yale UP, 1975.

Reichmann, Felix. *The Sources of Western Literacy: The Middle Eastern Civilizations.* Westport, CT: Greenwood, 1980.

Stock, Brian. *The Implications of Literacy: Written Language and Models of Interpretation in the Eleventh and Twelfth Centuries.* Princeton: Princeton UP, 1983.

Stone, Lawrence. *The Past and the Present.* Boston: Routledge and Kegan Paul, 1981.

Stubbs, Michael. *Language and Literacy.* London: Routledge and Kegan Paul, 1980.

Literary Composition

Altman, Joseph. *The Tudor Play of Mind: Rhetorical Inquiry and the Development of Elizabethan Drama.* Berkeley: U of California P, 1978.

Auerbach, Eric. *Literary Language and Its Public in Late Latin Antiquity and in the Middle Ages.* Trans. Ralph Manheim. Bollingen Series 74. New York: Pantheon, 1965.

Barthes, Roland. *Camera Lucida: Reflections on Photography.* Trans. Richard Howard. New York: Hill and Wang, 1981.

Burkhardt, Jacob. *The Civilization of the Renaissance in Italy.* Trans. S. G. C. Middlemore. 2nd ed. Oxford: Oxford UP, 1945.

Cavendish, Margaret. *The Life of William Cavendish, Duke of Newcastle.* Ed. C. H. Firth. 2nd ed., rev. London: George Routledge and Sons, n.d.

Chaytor, Henry. *From Script to Print: An Introduction to Medieval Literature.* Cambridge: Cambridge UP, 1945.

Coleman, Janet. *Medieval Readers and Writers, 1350–1400.* New York: Columbia UP, 1981.

Curtius, Ernst Robert. *European Literature and the Latin Middle Ages.* Trans. Willard R. Trask. Bollingen Series 36. Princeton: Princeton UP, 1973.

Fish, Stanley E. *Surprised by Sin: the Reader in Paradise Lost.* Berkeley: U of California P, 1971.

Freccero, John. "Autobiography and Narrative." *Reconstructing Individualism: Autonomy, Individuality, and the Self in Western Thought.* Ed. Thomas C. Heller, Morton Sosma, and David Wellbery. Stanford, CA: Stanford UP, 1986.

Havelock, Eric A. *Preface to Plato.* Cambridge, MA: Belknap, Harvard UP, 1963.

Hinman, Charlton. *The Printing and Proofreading of the First Folio of Shakespeare.* 2 vols. Oxford: Clarendon, 1963.

Holden, Jonathan. *The Rhetoric of the Contemporary Lyric.* Bloomington: Indiana UP, 1980.

Jonson, Ben. *Discoveries.* 1641. *Conversations with William Drummond of Hawthornden.* Ed. G. B. Harrison. *Elizabethan and Jacobean Quartos.* New York: Barnes and Noble, 1966.

———. *Discoveries: A Critical Edition with an Introduction and Notes on the True Purport and Genesis of the Book.* Ed. Maurice Catelain. Paris: Librairie Hachette and Cie, 1906.

———. *Timber.* Ed. G. B. Harrison. *Elizabethan and Jacobean Quartos.* New York: Barnes, 1966.

Kernan, Alvin. *Printing Technology, Letters and Samuel Johnson.* Princeton: Princeton UP, 1987.

Lanham, Richard. *Motives of Eloquence: Literary Rhetoric in the Renaissance.* New Haven: Yale UP, 1976.

Lord, Albert. *The Singer of Tales.* Harvard Studies in Comparative Literature 24. Cambridge, MA: Harvard UP, 1960.

McGann, Jerome. *Critique of Modern Textual Criticism.* Chicago: U of Chicago P, 1983.

Ong, Walter. "The Writer's Audience Is Always a Fiction." *PMLA* 90 (1975): 9–22.

Parrey, Milman. *The Making of Homeric Verse.* Oxford: Clarendon, 1971.

Poirier, Richard. *The Performing Self.* New York: Oxford UP, 1971.

Schragg, Calvin O. "Decentered Subjectivity and the New Humanism." Unpublished paper, 1981.

Yates, Frances. *The Art of Memory.* Harmondsworth: Penguin, 1969.

Literary Theory and Criticism

Barthes, Roland. *Image-Music-Text.* Trans. Stephen Heath. London: Hill and Wang, 1977.

——. *The Pleasures of the Text*. Trans. Richard Miller. New York: Hill and Wang, 1975.

——. *S/Z*. Trans. Richard Miller. Preface by Richard Howard. New York: Hill and Wang, 1974.

Bruns, Gerald L. *Inventions: Writing, Textuality and Understanding in Literary History*. New Haven: Yale UP, 1982.

Chadwick, Hector Mouro and Nora Kershaw Chadwick. *The Growth of Literature*. 3 vols. Cambridge: Cambridge UP, 1932–40.

Culler, Jonathan. *On Deconstruction: Theory and Criticism after Structuralism*. Ithaca, NY: Cornell UP, 1982.

——. *The Pursuit of Signs: Semiotics, Literature, Deconstruction*. Ithaca, NY: Cornell UP, 1981.

DeMan, Paul. *Allegories of Reading: Figural Language in Rousseau, Nietzsche, Rilke, and Proust*. New Haven: Yale UP, 1979.

——. "The Resistance to Theory." *The Pedagogical Imperative: Teaching as a Literary Genre*. Yale French Studies 63. Ed. Barbara Johnson. New Haven: Yale UP, 1982. 3–20.

Derrida, Jacques. *Dissemination*. Trans. Barbara Johnson. Chicago: U of Chicago P, 1981.

——. *Spurs: Nietzsche's Styles*. Trans. Barbara Harlow. Chicago: U of Chicago P, 1978.

Fish, Stanley. *Self-Consuming Artifacts*. Berkeley: U of California P, 1972.

Fletcher, Angus, ed. *The Literature of Fact: Selected Papers from the English Institute*. New York: Columbia UP, 1976.

Foucault, Michel. *Discipline and Punish: The Birth of the Prison*. Trans. Alan Sheridan. New York: Vintage, 1979.

——. "What Is an Author?" *Language, Counter-Memory, Practice*. Ed. Donald F. Bouchard. Trans. Donald Bouchard and Sherry Simon. Ithaca, NY: Cornell UP, 1977. 113–38.

Frye, Northrop. *Anatomy of Criticism: Four Essays*. Princeton: Princeton UP, 1957.

Genette, Gérard. "Rhétorique et Enseignement." *Figures II*. Paris: Éditions du Sevil, 1969. 23–42.

Greenblatt, Stephen. *Renaissance Self-Fashioning*. Chicago: U of Chicago P, 1980.

Grossman, Lionel. "The Fictions of Criticism." *Velocities of Change*. Ed. Richard Macksey. Baltimore: Johns Hopkins UP, 1974.

Guillory, John. *Poetic Authority: Spenser, Milton, and Literary History*. New York: Columbia UP, 1983.

Hartman, Geoffrey. *Saving the Text: Literature, Derrida, Philosophy*. Baltimore: Johns Hopkins UP, 1981.

Kermode, Frank. *The Genesis of Secrecy*. The Charles Eliot Norton Lectures. Cambridge, MA: Harvard UP, 1979.

Lentricchia, Frank. *After the New Criticism*. Chicago: U of Chicago P, 1980.

————. *Criticism and Social Change*. Chicago: U of Chicago P, 1983.

Lewis, C. S. *English Literature in the Sixteenth Century*. Oxford: Clarendon, 1954.

Minnis, A. J. *Medieval Theory of Authorship: Scholastic Literary Attitudes in the Later Middle Ages*. London: Scolar, 1984.

Preston, John. *The Created Self*. London: Heinemann, 1970.

Robinson, Forrest. *The Shape of Things Known*. Cambridge, MA: Harvard UP, 1971.

Shattuck, Roger. "How to Rescue Literature." *New York Review of Books* 27 (17 April 1980): 29–35.

Sidney, Sir Phillip. *An Apology for Poetry*. Ed. with introduction and notes by Forrest G. Robinson. Indianapolis: Bobbs, 1970.

Smith, G. Gregory. *Elizabethan Critical Essays*. 2 vols. Oxford: Oxford UP, 1946.

Stallybrass, Peter, and Allon White. *The Politics and Poetics of Transgression*. Ithaca, NY: Cornell UP, 1986.

Suleiman, Susan, and Inge Crosman, eds. *The Reader in the Text*. Princeton: Princeton UP, 1980.

Tompkins, Jane, ed. *Reader-Response Criticism*. Baltimore: Johns Hopkins UP, 1980.

Watt, Ian. *The Rise of the Novel*. Berkeley: U of California P, 1967.

Webber, Joan. *The Eloquent "I"*. Madison: U of Wisconsin P, 1968.

Wellek, René. *Concepts of Criticism*. Ed. with introduction by Stephen G. Nichols, Jr. New Haven: Yale UP, 1963.

Wellek, René, and Austin Warren. *A Theory of Literature*. 3rd ed. New York: Harcourt, 1956.

White, Hayden. *Metahistory: The Historical Imagination in Nineteenth-Century Europe*. Baltimore: Johns Hopkins UP, 1973.

Wimsatt, W. K., Jr., and Cleanth Brooks. *Literary Criticism: A Short History*. New York: Knopf, 1957.

Rhetoric: History and Theory

Anderson, Dorothy I. and Waldo W. Braden, eds. *Ellery T. Channing, Lectures Read to the Seniors at Harvard College*. Carbondale: Southern Illinois UP, 1968.

Aristotle. *Rhetoric*. Trans. Lane Cooper. New York: Appleton, 1932.

Augustine. *On Christian Doctrine; The Enchiridion*. Trans. J. F. Shaw. Edinburgh: T and T Clark, 1873.

————. *Writings of Saint Augustine*. Trans. Vernon J. Bourke. Vol. 15 of *Fathers of the Church*. Washington, DC: Catholic U of America P, 1953. 33 vols. to date. 1947–.

Bacon, Francis. *The Advancement of Learning*. Ed. James Spedding, Robert Leslie Ellis, and Douglas Denon Heath. New Edition. London: Longmans, et. al., 1876. Vol. 3 of *The Works of Francis Bacon*. 7 vols. 1876–83.

Bain, Alexander. *English Composition and Rhetoric*. 2nd ed. London: Longmans, 1869.

Berlin, James. *Rhetoric and Reality: Writing Instruction in American Colleges: 1900–1985*. Carbondale: Southern Illinois UP, 1987.

Bitzer, Lloyd. "The Rhetorical Situation." *Contemporary Theories of Rhetoric: Selected Readings*. Ed. Richard L. Johannesen. New York: Harper, 1971. 381–94.

Blair, Carole. "Nietzsche's Lecture Notes on Rhetoric: A Translation." *Philosophy and Rhetoric*. 16.2 (1983): 94–129.

Blair, Hugh. *Lectures on Rhetoric and Belles Lettres*. Ed. Harold F. Harding. 2 vols. Carbondale: Southern Illinois UP, 1965.

Booth, Wayne. "The Revival of Rhetoric." *PMLA* 80 (1965): 8–12.

Bowers, John Waite, and Robert E. Sanders. "Paradox as Rhetorical Strategy." *Rhetoric: A Tradition in Transition*. Ed. Walter R. Fisher. East Lansing: Michigan State UP, 1974. 299–315.

Burger, Ronna. *Plato's Phaedrus: A Defense of the Philosophical Art of Writing*. Tuscaloosa: U of Alabama P, 1980.

Burke, Kenneth. *Counter-Statement*. Berkeley: U of California P, 1968.

———. *The Philosophy of Literary Form*. Berkeley: U of California P, 1973.

———. *A Rhetoric of Motives*. Berkeley: U of California P, 1969.

Campbell, George. *The Philosophy of Rhetoric*. Ed. Lloyd F. Bitzer. Carbondale: Southern Illinois UP, 1963.

Cicero. [Cicero] *I*. Trans. H. Caplin. Ed. G. P. Goold. 2 vols. London: Loeb, 1981.

Connors, Robert. "Greek Rhetoric and the Transition from Orality." *Philosophy and Rhetoric* 19.1 (1986): 38–65.

Corder, Jim W. *Uses of Rhetoric*. Philadelphia: Lippincott, 1971.

Corts, Thomas E. "Special Report: The Derivation of Ethos." *Speech Monographs* 35 (1968): 201–2.

Cushman, Donald P. and Phillip K. Tomkins. "A Theory of Rhetoric for Contemporary Society." *Philosophy and Rhetoric* 23 (1980): 43–66.

Derrida, Jacques. *Margins of Philosophy*. Trans. Alan Bass. Chicago: U of Chicago P, 1982.

Dubois, Jacques, et al. *A General Rhetoric*. Trans. Paul B. Burrell and Edgar M. Stotkin. Baltimore: Johns Hopkins UP, 1981.

Erasmus, Desiderius. *De Copia*. (*On Copia of Words and Ideas*.) Trans. Donald B. King and H. David Rix. Milwaukee, WI: Marquette UP, 1963.

Fogarty, Daniel. *Roots for a New Rhetoric*. New York: Russell and Russell, 1959.

Forster, Edward S., ed. *Isocrates: Cyprian Orations*. New York: Arno, 1979.

Golden, James, Goodwin F. Berquist, and William E. Coleman. *The Rhetoric of Western Thought*. 3rd ed. Dubuque, IA: Kendall/Hunt, 1982.

Grimaldi, W. M. A., S. J. *Commentary on Aristotle's "Rhetoric I."* Fordham UP, 1980.

———. *Studies in the Philosophy of Aristotle's Rhetoric*. Hermes Einzelschriften 25. Wiesbaden: Steiner, 1972.

Guthrie, Warren. "The Development of Rhetorical Theory in America," pt. 1. *Speech Monographs* 13 (1946): 14–22.

———. "The Development of Rhetorical Theory in America: 1635–1850, 4." *Speech Monographs* 16 (1949): 98–113.

Halloran, S. Michael. "Rhetoric in the American College Curriculum: The Decline of Public Discourse." *Pre/Text* 3 (1982): 245–69.

Hobbes, Thomas. *The Whole Art of Rhetoric*. *The English Works of Thomas Hobbes of Malmesbury*. Ed. and coll. Sir William Molesworth Bart. Vol. 6. 1840. Aalen, Germany: Scientia, 1962.

Howell, Wilbur Samuel. *Eighteenth-Century British Logic and Rhetoric*. Princeton: Princeton UP, 1971.

Isocrates. Trans. George Norlin. 3 vols. Cambridge, MA: Harvard UP; London: Heinemann, 1928.

Jaeger, Werner. "The Rhetoric of Isocrates and Its Cultural Ideal." *The Province of Rhetoric*. Ed. Joseph Schwartz and John A. Rycinga. New York: Ronald, 1965. 84–111.

Kennedy, George. *The Art of Persuasion in Greece*. Princeton: Princeton UP, 1963.

———. *The Art of Rhetoric in the Roman World*. Princeton: Princeton UP, 1972.

———. *Classical Rhetoric and Its Christian and Secular Tradition from Ancient to Modern Times*. Chapel Hill: U of North Carolina P, 1980.

———. *Greek Rhetoric Under Christian Emperors*. Princeton: Princeton UP, 1983.

McKeon, Richard. "Rhetoric in the Middle Ages." *Spectrum* 7.1 (January 1942): 1–32.

———. "The Uses of Rhetoric in a Technological Age: Architechtonic Productive Arts." *The Prospect of Rhetoric*. Ed. Lloyd Bitzer and Edwin Black. Englewood Cliffs, NJ: Prentice-Hall, 1971. 44–63.

McNally, J. R. "Melanchthon's Earliest Rhetoric." *Rhetoric: A Tradition in Transition.* Ed. Walter R. Fisher. East Lansing: Michigan State UP, 1974. 33–48.

Murphy, James, ed. *Rhetoric in the Middle Ages: A History of Rhetorical Theory from St. Augustine to the Renaissance.* Berkeley: U of California P, 1974.

————. *A Synoptic History of Classical Rhetoric.* New York: Random House, 1972.

————, ed. *Three Medieval Rhetorical Arts.* Trans. James Murphy. Berkeley: U of California P, 1971.

Murrin, Michael. *The Veil of Allegory: Some Notes toward a Theory of Allegorical Rhetoric in the English Renaissance.* Chicago: U of Chicago P, 1969.

Nietzsche, Frederick. *Gesammelte Werke.* Munich: Musarion Verlag, 1922.

Ong, Walter. *Ramus, Method, and the Decay of Dialogue.* Cambridge, MA: Harvard UP, 1958.

————. "Tudor Writings on Rhetoric." *Studies in the Renaissance* 15 (1968): 39–69.

Perelman, Charles, and L. Olbrechts-Tyteca. *The New Rhetoric: A Treatise on Argumentation.* Trans. John Wilkinson and Purcell Weaver. Notre Dame: U of Notre Dame P, 1969.

Plato. *Gorgias.* Trans. with introduction by Walter Hamilton. Harmondsworth: Penguin, 1960.

————. *Phaedrus.* Trans. with introduction. by W. C. Helmbold and W. G. Robinowitz. Indianapolis: Bobbs-Merrill, 1956.

Quintilian. *Institutes.* Trans. H. E. Butler. Ed. G. P. Goold. 4 vols. London: Loeb, 1980.

Reid, Ronald F. "The Boylston Professorship of Rhetoric and Oratory, 1806–1904: A Case Study of Changing Concepts of Rhetoric and Pedagogy." *Quarterly Journal of Speech* 45 (1959): 239–57.

Richards, I. A. *Philosophy of Rhetoric.* London: Oxford UP, 1936.

Schwartz, Joseph, and John A. Rycinga, eds. *The Province of Rhetoric.* New York: Ronald, 1965.

Sennet, Richard. *The Fall of Public Man.* New York: Knopf, 1977.

Sheridan, Thomas. *A Course of Lectures on Elocution: Together with Two Dissertations on Language.* London: W. Strahan, 1762. New York: Benjamin Blom, 1968.

Sonnino, Lee A. *A Handbook to Sixteenth-Century Rhetoric.* London: Routledge and Kegan Paul, 1968.

Steinhoff, Virginia N. "The *Phaedrus* Idyll as Ethical Play: The Platonic Stance." *The Rhetorical Tradition and Modern Writing.* Ed. James J. Murphy. New York: MLA, 1982. 31–45.

Taylor, A. E. *Plato: The Man and His Work*. 7th ed. London: Methuen, 1960.

Tertullian. *Tertullian Against Praxeas*. Trans. A. Souter. London: n.p., 1920.

Toulmin, Stephen. *Human Understanding*. Vol. 1. Princeton: Princeton UP, 1972.

——. *The Uses of Argument*. Cambridge: Cambridge UP, 1958.

Vickers, Brian. Introduction. *Rhetoric Revalued: Papers from the International Society for the History of Rhetoric*. Medieval and Renaissance Texts and Studies. Binghamton, NY: Center for Medieval and Early Renaissance Studies, 1982.

Weaver, Richard. *The Ethics of Rhetoric*. Chicago: Regnery, 1953.

——. "Language Is Sermonic." *Contemporary Theories of Rhetoric: Selected Readings*. Ed. Richard L. Johannesen. New York: Harper, 1971.

Whately, Richard. *Elements of Rhetoric*. Ed. Douglas Ehringer. Carbondale: Southern Illinois UP, 1963.

Willard, Charles Arthur. "Argument Fields." *Advances in Argumentation Theory and Research*. Ed. Robert Cox and Charles Arthur Willard. Carbondale: Southern Illinois UP, 1982. 24–75.

Winterbottom, Michael. *Problems in Quintilian*. BICS Supplement. Vol. 25. London: U of London, 1970.

Index

Alphabet: as discourse paradigm, 59,57,85,122; as writing technology, 54, 56, 122

Aristotle, 14, 31, 23, 32, 40, 62, 74, 75, 102, 133, 155; on forgery, 75; *Gryllus*, 58; *Rhetoric*, 59, 119, 129; in Whately, 135

Assignments, 48, 160, 166. *See also* Examinations; Teaching practices

Audience, 14, 122; as "time," 144; Universal, 95, 145–46

Auerbach, Eric, 84, 86

Augustine Saint, 6, 21, 72, 73, 79, 128, 147; *On Christian Doctrine*,129–31

Austin, Gilbert, 77

Author(s), 3, 12; absence from texts, 139; death of, 14; not students, 150; privileged, 52; univocal, 32, 100 167, 168. *See also* Blake, William; Writers

Authorial (secondary) literacy, 80–89, 97, 134, 166

Authority: as "authoritative view," 146, 147; becomes authenticity, 83, 98; deference to, 166; of texts, 74–76, 79,87, 130

Authorship, 3, 5, 39, 53, 169; copyright, 86; establishment of, 93–99, 100; French parallels to English development of, 180 n.4; identity of writer, 100; individual, 83; medieval, 72–73, 81; of novel, 97; Renaissance vernacular, 85–89, 92–97. *See also* Blake, William; Ong, Walter

Bacon, Francis, 29, 75, 85, 90, 147; *Advancement of Learning*, 134, 135

Bain, Alexander, 136–38, 141, 152, 161

Baldwin, Charles Sears, 154

Barthes, Roland, 33–34

Bartholomae, David, 7, 166–67, 169

Basic writer, 151, 163–70

Berlin, James, 163

Blair, Hugh, 21, 134–35, 160

Blake, William: as "author," 16–17

Bonaventura, Saint, 72

Booth, Wayne, 51

Boylston Chair of Rhetoric, 155–56

Bruns, Gerald, 34–36, 39

Burckhardt, Jacob, 82

Burger, Rhona, 122

Burke, Kenneth, 35, 140; definitions of rhetoric, 143–45; dramatic ratios, 148; "timely" topic, 144

Campbell, Geroge, 33, 134–35, 160

Campion, Thomas, 85

Cave, Terrance, 132

Channing, Ellery T., 150, 155, 156–59, 160, 163

Charlemagne, 77

Chaytor, Henry, 58

Child, Francis, 160

Cicero, 64, 67–68, 132–33

Clanchy, M. T., 58, 76

Commonplace book(s), 62, 154; Ben Jonson's, 86

Communication anxiety, 160

Composing processes, 20, 42, 79; in Channing, 158; history of, 176 n.17; medieval, 71, 73; oral theories, 127; in Quintilian, 67–71; variability of, 9, 71–72

196

Susan Miller is the author of *Writing: Process and Product*, *The Written World*, and numerous theoretical and historical articles about composition and rhetoric. She has directed composition at Ohio State University, the University of Wisconsin-Milwaukee, and the University of Utah, where she is a faculty member in the English department, the university writing program, and educational studies.